CW00429054

RALPH STORER is an experienced h
sively around the world. Althougl
lived in Scotland since studying psychology at Dundee University
and has a great affinity for the Highlands. As well as disappearing
into the hills for a regular fix of nature, he also writes novels and
non-fiction, and produces darkwave music on his home computer.

His writing is known for its witty take on matters mountainous
and his guidebooks have become standard works on the subject.

*His books are exceptional... Storer subverts the guidebook genre
completely.* THE ANGRY CORRIE

THE ULTIMATE GUIDE TO THE MUNROS series
... picks up where others – including my own – leave off.
CAMERON MCNEISH

*Fabulously illustrated... Entertaining as well as informative...
One of the definitive guides to the Munros.* PRESS & JOURNAL

*Irresistibly funny and useful; an innovatively thought-through
guidebook that makes an appetising broth of its wit, experience
and visual and literary tools. Brilliant.* OUTDOOR WRITERS &
PHOTOGRAPHERS GUILD

*With the winning combination of reliable advice and
quirky humour, this is the ideal hillwalking companion.*
SCOTS MAGAZINE

*While most climbing authors appear to have had their funny
bones removed, Storer is happy to share numerous irreverent
insights into the hills.* SCOTTISH FIELD

As fun as it is practical. EDINBURGH EVENING NEWS

BAFFIES' EASY MUNRO GUIDE series
*Packed to bursting with concise information and route descrip-
tions. There should be room for this guide in every couch potato's
rucksack.* OUTDOOR WRITERS & PHOTOGRAPHERS GUILD

A truly outstanding guidebook. UNDISCOVERED SCOTLAND

*It is perfect for anyone exploring Scotland's beautiful mountains,
whatever his or her level of experience.* GUIDEPOST

50 CLASSIC ROUTES ON SCOTTISH MOUNTAINS
*The book begs to be picked up and thumbed through.
It will stimulate walkers to head for the hills.* TIMES
EDUCATIONAL SUPPLEMENT

50 BEST ROUTES ON SKYE AND RAASAY
*What an excellent book. As comprehensive a guide to walking
and scrambling on Skye as you could wish for.* HIGH

THE JOY OF HILLWALKING
A treat for all hillwalkers active or chairbound.
SCOTS INDEPENDENT

50 SHADES OF HILLWALKING
A fantastic celebration of this addictive pastime. SCOTLAND
OUTDOORS

SEE YOU ON THE HILL
*If you read one book about hillwalking this year, read this one…
a classic in the making.* UNDISCOVERED SCOTLAND

THE ULTIMATE MOUNTAIN TRIVIA QUIZ CHALLENGE
*A thoroughly fascinating way to kill time – every bothy should be
furnished with one.* THE SCOTSMAN

100 BEST ROUTES ON SCOTTISH MOUNTAINS

BAFFIES' GREAT OUTDOORS INAPPROPRIATE GLOSSARY

BAFFIES' GREAT OUTDOORS INAPPROPRIATE ADVICE
COLUMN

Corrour Bothy

A Refuge in the Wilderness

RALPH STORER

Luath Press Limited

EDINBURGH

www.luath.co.uk

For bothy companions

Hillwalking and mountaineering are not risk-free activities and may prove injurious to users of this book. While every care and effort has been taken in its preparation, readers should note that information contained within may not be accurate and can change following publication. Neither the publisher nor the author accept any liability for injury or damage of any kind arising directly or indirectly from the book's contents.

First published 2020

ISBN: 978-1-913025-56-4

The paper used in this book is recyclable. It is made from low chlorine pulps produced in a low energy, low emission manner from renewable forests.

Printed and bound by Ashford Colour Press, Gosport

Typeset in 10.5 point Sabon by Lapiz

The author's right to be identified as author of this work under the Copyright, Designs and Patents Act 1988 has been asserted.

© Ralph Storer 2020

Amid the Grampian mountains wild,
Where silence reigns supreme,
And nought disturbs the solitude,
Except the rushing stream,
There stands a lonely windswept house
Of no pretentious size.
But to the hail-slung mountaineer
It's perfect paradise.
No architectural beauties
Its crude grey walls adorn,
Yet wide its hospitable door
To high and lowly born.
Though meagre its capacities
Conveniences but few,
Its form is dear to all mankind
Who cross the Lairig Ghru.

Anonymous, 14 July 1939
Corrour Visitors' Book Vol 8

ACKNOWLEDGEMENTS

THE CONSIDERABLE RESEARCH required for this book would have been impossible without the generous help given to me by many people: the staff of the Dundee University Archives (where nearly all known Corrour Bothy visitors' books are now held), the AK Bell Library in Perth, the National Library of Scotland and the University of Edinburgh Library; Dominic Shann, Fiona Eardley and others at Scottish Natural Heritage, who helped to source other volumes of the visitors' books and relocate them to Dundee; Mike Watson, John Higham and others at the Scottish Mountaineering Club, who also helped to source material.

Particular thanks to Innes Ewen, who allowed his father William's archive of photographic material to be deposited in the Dundee University Archives and used in this book.

I am particularly indebted to Neil Reid, MBA trustee, Corrour Bothy maintenance officer at the time of writing and author of the cairngormwanderer blog. Neil has provided unstinting support, corrected errors and been patient at answering a seemingly endless succession of queries.

Finally, my thanks to all those bothiers, both named and unnamed in the text, who have recorded their thoughts in the visitors' books. Their entries span a century of life at Corrour and have made this book possible.

ABBREVIATIONS USED IN TEXT

CCJ   Cairngorm Club Journal
MBA   Mountain Bothies Association
NNR   National Nature Reserve
NTS   National Trust for Scotland
SMCJ   Scottish Mountaineering Club Journal
SNH   Scottish Natural Heritage

CONTENTS

CORROUR THROUGH EXPERIENCE

SETTING THE SCENE

THE CAIRNGORMS

THE CAIRNGORMS FORM the largest tract of high country in Britain, with more land over 1200m/4000ft, 900m/3000ft and 600m/2000ft (over 200 square miles of it) than anywhere else. Five of Britain's six highest mountains are found here – only Ben Nevis is higher. They're named after the sixth highest – Cairn Gorm – because that's the one that is most prominent when viewed from Aviemore on the main north-south thoroughfare through Strathspey.

Ironically, the name means Blue Mountains, but in Gaelic they are more properly called Am Monadh Ruadh (*Am Monna Roo-a*, The Red Mountains), named for the pink colour of their granite. This contrasts with the mica-schists of Am Monadh Liath (*Am Monna Lee-a*, The Grey Mountains) on the other side of Aviemore across Strathspey.

Geographically, they form a series of great plateaus split by deep, glaciated U-shaped glens, which give hillwalkers and climbers access to the range's remote recesses. Their height gives the plateaus an arctic-like environment, complete with appropriate flora and fauna whose biodiversity conservationists fight to maintain against increasing human leisure demands.

The scale is monumental. The plateau rims are scalloped by huge secret corries and cliff faces that have wow factor to spare. Add to this the rugged wildness, long lonely glens, hidden lochs and lochans… Walking in such country can become addictive.

The high plateaus are split into three groups by two major north-south glen-systems: the Lairig Ghru and the Lairig an Laoigh. The former is a great corridor that runs for 20 miles between the 4,000ft peaks, linking Speyside (Aviemore) in the north to Deeside (Braemar) in the south. It is the finest mountain pass in Britain.

'Lairig' (*Lahrik*) is the Gaelic name for a mountain pass. 'Ghru' is often said to be derived from the Gaelic *Ghruamach* (*Ghrooamach*, Gloomy), but more likely it is an aspirated form of Druidh (*Droo-y*, Flowing), as the Allt Druidh is the stream on the north side of the pass. Much restoration work has been done on the ancient path at both ends, but the stony wilderness of the upper Lairig remains much as it ever was.

> The Larig (Ghru) is one of the most remarkable glens in the district, and the Cairngorms cannot be considered 'done' until it has been traversed.
> Alex Inkson McConnochie, *Ben Muich Dhui and his neighbours*, 1885

The pass has a long history. Warring clans used it for incursions into enemy territory. In 1527, the Grants of Rothiemurchus on the north side marched through it to slaughter the Shaws of Deeside on the south side. During the Civil War of the 1640s, the Earl of Montrose marched an army through it, losing a canon to the bog on the way. Until the 1870s, northern drovers herded their cattle through it to the trysts and markets further south, although the Lairig an Laoigh (*Loo-y*, Pass of the Calves) to the east was more popular as it was less rugged. Every spring the upper stretches of the Lairig Ghru had to be cleared of rocks brought down by winter storms.

It is the at the heart of the Lairig Ghru, on the south side of the summit, at an altitude of 560m/1,800ft, far from any road, that Corrour Bothy is located.

THE SCOTTISH BOTHY

MOUNTAIN HUTS ARE a feature of many of the world's mountain ranges, but the bothies of the Scottish Highlands are unique. Many mountain huts in the High Alps are well-appointed, purpose-built, fee-paying establishments that offer overnight accommodation half-way up mountains in order to make climbs and summit bids possible. There's no need for such a hut system for the UK's lower mountain ranges, although a few private huts run by clubs such as the Scottish Mountaineering Club do exist in useful locations here and there, such as at the foot of the North Face of Ben Nevis. What the Scottish Highlands do have, however, is a patchwork of old buildings that date from a time when the glens were more populated than they are today.

A tumultuous history, punctuated with clan warfare, famines and evictions, saw the Highlands cleared of much of the population in the 18th and 19th centuries, and this left countless buildings empty. Most have now been dismantled or have fallen to ruin. Anyone who has walked in the Highlands will be familiar with the broken walls and foundations that still dot the Highland landscape.

A counter-trend in some areas saw numbers of farm workers increasing in the wake of the agricultural revolution and numbers of estate workers increasing to service the great sporting estates of the 19th century. These workers were housed in what was known as a bothan, the Gaelic word for hut, anglicised to bothy. Some were stand-alone buildings, others were built as an annex to the farmhouse. They were usually of no more than basic construction and in time most of these, too, fell into disuse or ruin.

One worker from the 1850s described his bothy as 'a hut resembling a pighouse'. Another later recalled '24 men crowded in a rusty corn-kiln, open from gable to gable and not above 30 feet in length'. Another remembered telling the time at night by stars seen through the gaps in the roof.

Today, all old buildings that survive in the wild solidly enough to still provide basic shelter are known as bothies. Some walkers now seek them out as others bag Munros, in a pursuit that has become known as bothying. There are also a number of more dilapidated shelters, cobbled together from bits of old building material or formed by caves or large boulders, known as howfs.

Most bothies provide no more than Spartan refuge, often with little furniture in them besides a table and a bench or chair. But they provide shelter and can save lives. Most can only be reached on foot or by mountain bike. Of the few that can be reached by vehicle, approach tracks are closed to the public. If this wasn't the case, many bothies would by now probably have been subjected to vandalism, which is unfortunately an ongoing problem for public buildings in remote places without a custodian.

In 1965, a group of bothy enthusiasts got together to form the Mountain Bothies Association (MBA, www.mountainbothies.org. uk), a voluntary group that, with landowners' permission, renovates and maintains bothies to make them habitable. Not all bothies are looked after by the MBA, but more than 100 are, with the vast majority in Scotland, including Corrour.

In addition to Corrour, there are several other bothies dotted around the Cairngorms, such as Ryvoan in the Lairig an Laoigh and Ruigh Aiteachain in Glen Feshie. Until recent times, they were little known outside the outdoor community. With the spread of information via the internet and social media, their locations became more widely known and in 2009 the MBA decided to share the fruits of its work by publishing a list of bothies online. Some still disagree with this move. In 2015, to celebrate its 50th anniversary, the organisation received the Queen's Award for Voluntary Service.

In living memory there used to be even more bothies and howfs in the Cairngorms. After the Second World War, the military built high-level shelters on the plateaus. More substantial bothies existed in the Lairig Ghru on the flanks of Braeriach (the Sinclair Hut at NH 959037) and in Coire an Lochain on the far side of Braeriach

(Jean's Hut at NH 981034). Following accidents and tragedies in which people died while searching for shelter, and through deterioration, all these had been abandoned or demolished by the early 1990s. Now only lower-level bothies such as Corrour remain in the Cairngorms.

CORROUR BOTHY

CORROUR BOTHY (NN 981958) is the most famous bothy of all and perhaps the oldest still in use. Sited at the foot of the rocky monolith known as The Devil's Point, at a height of 564m/1,850ft, it occupies a prime position at the heart of some of the wildest country in the Highlands.

The bothy is named for the corrie behind it – Coire Odhar. 'Odhar' means dun-coloured or brownish-grey, which describes many a Highland corrie's appearance. There's even another Coire Odhar close by, in Gleann Eanaich on the far side of the plateau to the west. There's another further west that, to the confusion of many visitors, gives its name to a station on the West Highland railway line. 'Odhar' is pronounced as in 'lower', not 'hour', hence *Corr-oa-ar*, anglicised to Corrour. The 'dh' in Gaelic is silent.

In former times, cattle were grazed in Coire Odhar during the summer months and there are remains of shielings (farmers' huts) in the vicinity of the bothy. As far as we know, the original bothy was built in 1877, during the heyday of the great sporting estates. Its purpose was to house a deer watcher, who would keep an eye on deer movements for the benefit of paying guests during the stalking season. After the last watcher left his lonely outpost in 1920, the bothy was locked and abandoned by the landowner (Mar Lodge Estate), but travellers were soon using it as a shelter or base and in 1928 it acquired its first visitors' book.

The importance of Corrour's location was highlighted in 1995 when the estate was purchased by the National Trust for Scotland, with Scottish Natural Heritage as an active partner in estate management. In 2017, it was designated the UK's largest National Nature Reserve.

As the years passed and Cairngorm storms wreaked havoc, the fabric of the bothy deteriorated, not least because its interior was stripped of wood to feed the fire. In 1950 the building was reconstructed by members of the Cairngorm Club and others and in 1959 a footbridge was built over the Dee to enable access from the Lairig Ghru path without a ford of the river. These improvements, together with the growth of hillwalking as a leisure activity, further increased the bothy's popularity during the latter decades of the 20th century. The designation of the Cairngorms as a national park in 2003 encouraged even more traffic.

By then the bothy was being maintained, as it still is, by the Mountain Bothies Association and in 2006 members undertook a second reconstruction of the building. Improvements included a wooden floor, panelling, insulation and a small sleeping platform. To eliminate the environmental hazard of accumulating human waste, an extension was added containing a composting toilet.

Corrour Bothy's single 6x3.6m room is now 'cosy' and often busy, which makes it even more cosy. Even if you intend to stay the night, it is wise to take a tent in case the place is crowded. In the surviving visitors' books, the largest number to have stayed the night is 20 in July 1956. The volume of traffic can be gauged from the fact that, in 2018, the toilet extension had to be rebuilt with more seats. Many now prefer the privacy of wild camping nearby, in the sure knowledge that the bothy will provide its customary sanctuary in case of emergency.

BOTHY PROTOCOLS

THE MBA BOTHY CODE with respect to Corrour:

Respect the bothy

- Don't leave graffiti or vandalise the bothy in any way.
- Pack out all rubbish. Don't leave it or bury it. It's ok to leave unopened tins behind for others but don't leave perishable food. It attracts vermin.
- Make sure the door and all windows are properly closed, otherwise deer and other wild animals can find their way in.
- If you build a fire, make sure it's completely extinguished before you leave.
- Leave the bothy as you would wish to find it: clean and tidy.

Respect other users

- ...even if you wish they weren't there.
- Avoid anti-social behaviour.
- Leave dry kindling and fuel for others if you have any spare.
- Remember that the bothy is the only shelter for miles around, so there is ALWAYS room for one more.

Respect the surroundings

- Don't pollute the bothy and its surroundings with rubbish and human waste. Observe instructions for use of the toilet.
- There are no trees and no fuel in the surrounding area. If you intend to build a fire, carry in your own supply of fuel. Do *not* attempt to dig up bogwood.
- Don't wash, wash up or brush teeth in the River Dee. If you do use river water for ablutions, empty waste water downriver of the bothy well away from the bank.

- Water can be obtained from a small stream 50m north of the bothy. It is rare to contract an infection from drinking Highland stream water, but for extra reassurance in the vicinity of human accommodation you may wish to boil or filter it before drinking.

Respect agreement with the estate

- Use the bothy as temporary accommodation for short stays only.
- If the bothy is vandalised or misused it may be closed to the public, as others have been.

Respect the restriction on numbers

- The MBA stipulates that no single party should have more than six members without permission from the landowner. Large groups preclude use by others and cause environmental problems.
- Commercial groups are not permitted.

Finally

- Do make a coruscatingly brilliant entry in the visitors' book for future generations to enjoy.

WALKING TO CORROUR

AS CORROUR LIES at the heart of the Lairig Ghru, it can be reached from either end of the pass. From the north (OS Land-ranger map 36), the easiest of several roadside starting points is Whitewell, at the end of a minor road 3 miles south-east of Aviemore (Route 1a). From here, the walk to Corrour is 11 miles long and crosses the 835m/2,740ft summit of the pass – an ascent of 550m/1,800ft on the way in and 285m/935ft on the way out. A shorter but more awkward approach begins at the Sugarbowl car park on the road to Coire Cas ski slopes (Route 1b).

From the south (OS Landranger map 43), the nearest roadside starting point is Linn of Dee, 7 miles west of Braemar (Route 2a). From here, the walk to Corrour via Derry Lodge is 8 miles long, with only 230m/750ft of ascent on the way in and 60m/200ft on the way out, making it by far the most popular approach. Not only is it shorter and requires less ascent in both directions, but also tracks and paths are better surfaced and the route is arguably the more scenic of the two. As with the northern approach, there's a shorter but more awkward variation via White Bridge (Route 2b).

Route 1a: the northern (Aviemore) approach from Whitewell (NH 915287)

From Whitewell a path leads 200m down to a wider cycle track that runs for 80m to a crossroads. The track to the Lairig Ghru turns left here, running deep into Rothiemurchus Forest to cross a river (footbridge) and reach a junction 2 miles from Whitewell. The Lairig Ghru path goes right here. In its lower reaches, much of it has been upgraded, but there are still some rough sections higher up.

Once out of the trees the path enters the narrow, deep-cut glen of the Allt Druidh between the massive slopes of Braeriach and the Cairn Gorm-Ben Macdui plateau. The stream disappears underground and the ascent steepens onto the extensive summit boulderfield of the pass at a height of 833m/2733ft, where the four Pools of Dee lie in hollows among the boulders.

The path undulates and twists around the pools before descending the U-shaped trench of Glen Dee amid increasingly imposing surroundings. After passing the gaping entrance to An Garbh Choire, the angle eases and, with the twin conical sentinels of Carn a' Mhaim and The Devil's Point facing each other across the Dee to draw you on, it's now not much further to Corrour.

Route 1b: the northern (Aviemore) approach from the Sugarbowl (NH 985075)

You can save 1½ miles each way on the northern approach by beginning at the Sugarbowl car park on the road to Coire Cas ski slopes, but it's a much more awkward approach. It involves clambering through the giant boulder-jam that fills the Chalamain Gap to join the Lairig Ghru path at the foot of Braeriach.

Walkers are lured by the Sugarbowl's high starting point (150m/500ft higher than Whitewell) but, as well as a slow clamber through the gap, you'll lose 100m/330ft of height on the descent to the Lairig. The route is popular for ascents of Braeriach with a light day sack, but if walking to Corrour with a larger pack many will find the Whitewell approach less aggravating. Whether you find the clamber through the Chalamain Gap fun or awkward is a question of preference, but few relish the climb back up to it from the Lairig on the return trip.

Route 2a: the southern (Braemar) approach from Linn of Dee (NO 064898) via Derry Lodge

From Linn of Dee car park (toilets; small parking fee), a path joins a Land Rover track that runs 3 miles up tranquil Glen Lui to Derry Lodge. Just beyond the lodge, a footbridge across the Derry Burn gives access to a path that continues west along Glen Luibeg. The path crosses grassy riverside flats and cuts a scenic swathe through pinewoods to the Luibeg Burn, just before which it forks. The left branch crosses the stream on stepping stones. The right branch detours to a bridge 400m upstream.

On the far side the path climbs 230m/750ft around the flanks of Carn a' Mhaim, passing a right branch to the summit of the Munro. It then becomes more bouldery and often wetter on a 60m/200ft descent to the River Dee, but the scenery improves dramatically as the striking peak of The Devil's Point looms into view.

On approach to the river, the path forks. The right branch continues through the Lairig Ghru to Aviemore. The left branch crosses the river by footbridge to reach the bothy.

Situated amid fine stands of old Scots pines, the grand edifice of Derry Lodge was originally an 18th-century single-story building used for recreational hunting and fishing. It was enlarged several times in the 19th century and in its heyday played host to many important guests. Queen Victoria is said to have dropped in for a cup of tea following her ascent of Ben Macdui in 1859 and King Edward VII came for the shooting in 1905. During the Second World War it was a military training base for mountain warfare and after that it was leased by the Cairngorm Club, which allowed vehicle access from Linn of Dee for two shillings and sixpence (12½p). Since the club gave up the lease in 1967, the building has been damaged by vandalism and fire. The National Trust for Scotland maintains a waterproof exterior shell while discussions about its future continue (see Page 88).

Route 2b: the southern (Braemar) approach from Linn of Dee (NO 064898) via White Bridge

A second route to Corrour from Linn of Dee follows the River Dee all the way. It goes west along a Land Rover track for 3 miles to White Bridge then follows a path along the river's east (right-hand) bank to join the Derry Lodge route 120m before the junction at which the Corrour path branches left to the footbridge.

Compared to the Derry Lodge route, the White Bridge route adds around an extra mile to the trip and can be boggy beyond the bridge, but it does reduce the ascent by 60m/200ft both on the way in and the way out. It is also arguably more scenic, with The Devil's Point as constant backdrop and, at the Chest of Dee especially, some fine waterfalls and pools on the river. Many visit Corrour by combining the two routes, using one for the walk-in and the other for the walk-out.

Note also that, beyond White Bridge, a much better path (a rewilded former vehicle track) runs along the west (left-hand) bank of the Dee for 3½ miles to end near a lochan at NN 987918. This gives much easier walking than the east-bank path but, after it ends, there's still 2½ miles to go to Corrour across boggy ground at the mouth of Glen Geusachan, including a ford of the considerable Geusachan Burn. The only way to avoid this section is to ford the Dee to pick up the east-bank path, but the Dee can be deceptively deep and fast-flowing. Any attempt to ford it is inadvisable except at low water and by experienced walkers.

Notes for Mountain Bikers

Reaching Corrour can be made easier by using a mountain bike part-way. On the northern approach, the initial track to the Lairig Ghru junction in the forest gives an enjoyable and virtually level ride (2 miles). Although the pass has a long history of 'cycling', any attempt to continue further will require large amounts of pushing owing to gradient and terrain, including tree roots, rocks and scree.

The southern approach can be cycled easily to Derry Lodge (3 miles), even if the undulating track requires effort in places. More technically, with cross drains across the path, you can ride as far as the Luibeg Burn (4½ miles).

The alternative White Bridge route can be cycled easily to White Bridge (3 miles). The excellent path on the west-bank path of the Dee can also be cycled for a further 3½ miles and would be easy were it not for the profusion of cross-drains. At its end, however, as noted above, you're then faced with a ford of the Dee or a boggy 2½-mile walk that includes a crossing of the Geusachan Burn.

Foul Weather Considerations

After rain, sections of the Lairig Ghru path act as channels for water from the mountainsides above. On the northern approach,

this is especially true on the descent from the summit of the pass
into Glen Dee. The stony path at the summit of the pass itself can
be hard to follow in cloud, especially if under snow. Of course, no
one should attempt to get to Corrour under snow without winter
experience. On the southern approach via Derry Lodge, the path
channels water on the descent from the shoulder of Carn a' Mhaim
into Glen Dee.

In low cloud or darkness, note that the bridge over the Dee to
Corrour lies 300m south-east of the bothy, and the cairned junction of the path to it from the Lairig Ghru path lies a further 200m
south-east of the bridge (NN 985955).

The White Bridge route is best avoided in wet conditions. Beyond
the bridge, whether you take the east-side or west-side route beside
the Dee, you'll eventually be faced with very boggy ground and a
difficult crossing of either the Dee or the Geusachan Burn.

Other Options

There are many more adventurous ways of reaching Corrour, as recorded in the visitors'
books. Before private car
ownership, a popular one- to
two-day approach was from
Blair Atholl station via Glen
Tilt or Glen Fealar to White
Bridge. Others come from
Glen Feshie to the west over
the Moine Mor and down
Glen Geusachan. Others come
from Gleann Eanaich over the
Western Cairngorms Plateau.

> The Shelter Stone (Clach Dhion
> in Gaelic), once measured to be
> 44x21x22ft high, is the largest of
> many massive boulders lying at the
> foot of the crag named after it at
> the head of Loch Avon. Although the
> space beneath it isn't high enough to
> stand up in, it can sleep five or six
> easily. Once a howf for thieves, it was
> here, on the night of Queen Victoria's
> Golden Jubilee, that the Cairngorm
> Club was founded in 1887.

Others arrive at Corrour unsure which way they've come.

Another adventurous approach is over the Central Cairngorms Plateau from the Shelter Stone in the Loch Avon basin. This
approach is not recommended to inexperienced walkers as it ends
with a very steep and rough descent into the Lairig Ghru. The easiest
way down is via the Ben Macdui–Carn a' Mhaim bealach, reached

by descending the awkward boulderfield of Macdui's south-west spur. From here, if you can find it, a rough path descends to the Lairig. It's also possible to descend from Macdui to the Lairig Ghru more directly via the March Burn or the Tailors' Burn (Allt Clach nan Taillear), but these routes are even steeper and tougher and require more care.

WALKING FROM CORROUR

THE FOLLOWING IS intended to give no more than an overview of the walking possibilities available at Corrour and is not meant to be a definitive guide. For full details of these routes and others, including more exciting scrambles, see the author's *The Ultimate Guide to the Munros Volume 5: Cairngorms North*.

Lairig Ghru west side

The rocky arrowhead peak of The Devil's Point (1,004m/3,294ft), the most striking mountain in the Cairngorms, looms over Corrour and is an obvious objective. Although it looks impossible to climb from most angles, there is in fact an easy way up via the corrie that gives Corrour its name. From the bothy a renovated path climbs to a hidden saddle on the mountain's north-west side, and from here it's only a short walk to the summit.

The Devil's Point lies at the south end of the Western Cairngorms Plateau, which stretches northwards along the west side of the Lairig across Cairn Toul (1,291m/4,236ft) and Sgor an Lochain Uaine (1,258m/4,127ft, sometimes jokingly called Angel's Peak) to Braeriach (1,296m/4,252ft). A round trip across the plateau, crossing the four Munros, is a classic day walk from Corrour. It's best done by climbing Braeriach first and leaving the Coire Odhar path for an easy descent at the end of the day. Walkers will have to cross the summit of the Lairig Ghru to pick up the Braeriach ascent path at the foot of Chalamain Gap, but scramblers can take a short cut up its south-east ridge on the rim of Coire Bhrochain.

Lairig Ghru east side

Carn a' Mhaim (1,037m/3,403ft) faces The Devil's Point across the Lairig and makes an equally attractive objective. The normal ascent path climbs the southern slopes, beginning just above the Luibeg

Burn and passed on the walk-in to Corrour from Linn of Dee via
Derry Lodge. The ascent from Corrour via the mountain's north
ridge is more interesting. The ridge is unique in the Cairngorms
for its narrowness, but it's completely without difficulty, with only
one brief rocky section that doesn't even require a scramble. From
the Lairig Ghru a rough side path climbs to the bealach at its foot,
between Carn a' Mhaim and Ben Macdhui.

Carn a' Mhaim lies at the south end of the Central Cairngorms
Plateau, which extends northwards along the east side of the Lairig
over Ben Macdui to Cairn Gorm. Unfortunately, it's less amenable
to day hikes from Corrour than its equivalent on the west side of
the Lairig. Cairn Gorm is distant while the western slopes of Macdui that drop to the Lairig are massive and steep.

The only easy breach in the slopes is the bealach just mentioned.
Ben Macdui's summit lies directly above it, but the ascent from
there involves negotiating over 500m of steep, penitential boulderfield on the south-west spur. There's nothing technically difficult
about the ascent, but a tendency to masochism is of great benefit
to its enjoyment. The easiest way down is to reverse the route.
There *are* other ways down, via the Tailors' Burn and March Burn,
but they're even steeper and could lead to difficulty.

Other day walks

On the west side of the River Dee south of Corrour, two more
remote Munros are accessible from the west-bank path above
White Bridge: Beinn Bhrotain (1,157m/3,796ft) and Monadh Mor
(1,113m/3,652ft). They're an awkward pair to reach from any
starting point, but a round from Corrour that returns via the gaping trench of Glen Geusachan gives an adventurous walk on the
wild side.

Above Derry Lodge, Derry Cairngorm (1,155m/3,790ft) is a
lone Munro that is normally tackled as a day walk from Linn of
Dee. But it could also be climbed en route to or from Corrour.

On the east side of the Dee, between the White Bridge route and the
Derry Lodge route, is a great tract of little-explored country whose
highpoint is the Corbett of Sgor Mor (Big Peak, 813m/2,667ft).
Approached by its SSE ridge from Glen Dee, its ascent gives a walk

that finishes up smooth granite blocks and slabs to grandstand views
of The Devil's Point and the Lairig.

Shorter Walks

For shorter days, instead
of climbing the mountains
around the bothy, it's worth
taking time out to explore the
Lairig and its massive corries.
Wander up Coire Odhar to
see the attractive water-slide
at its back. Explore the mouth
of Glen Geusachan (*Gyoosa-
chan*, Little Pine Wood), one
of the greatest trenches in the
Highlands. Visit the Tailors'

> The Tailors' Stone's name derives
> from a legend of three tailors. One
> Hogmanay, they had drunkenly
> boasted that on a single winter's
> day they could dance a reel in
> Abernethy and Rothiemurchus to
> the north as well as in Mar to the
> south. Alas, they fell foul of a Lairig
> blizzard and perished while seeking
> shelter at their eponymous stone.

Stone, the largest and flattest of a group of rocks on the right of the
Lairig Ghru path a short distance to the north.

Beyond here, you can continue northwards to visit the Pools of
Dee at the summit of the Lairig. The four beautifully clear pools,
two large and two small, lie in hollows among the boulders. They
are connected underground and water can just be detected seeping
in and out of their ends. They are said never to freeze over, which is
difficult to believe given the volume of snow that is often dumped
here each winter. The old name for the pools was Lochan Dubh na
Lairige (Black Lochans of the Pass) and it is a shame that this more
vivid and evocative name has been superseded.

For the best rock scenery, follow the Dee west into massive Garbh
Coire (in Gaelic An Garbh Choire, *Garrav Chorra*, The Rough Corrie), marvel at the surrounding rock architecture, visit the small
restored refuge at NN 959986 and perhaps continue up past Braeriach's Coire Bhrochain (*Vrochin*, Porridge) to the two high inner corries beneath the headwall. To the right is Garbh Choire Dhaidh (a
map error for Dhé, *Yay*, meaning Dee). To the left is Garbh Choire
Mor (*Moar*, Big) with its semi-permanent snowbeds (see Page 162).

Or... on a fine summer's day there's much to be said for simply lounging outside the bothy, soaking up the atmosphere of the
Lairig and planning future adventures.

THE VISITORS' BOOKS

Book	Volume	Start date	End date
1	Vol 1	27 Jun 1928	12 Sep 1929
2	Vol 2	12 Sep 1929	12 Apr 1931
3	Vol 3	12 Apr 1931	19 Jun 1932
4	Vol 6	1 Jul 1935	13 Jun 1937
5	Vol 7	13 Jun 1937	30 Jul 1938
6	Vol 8	23 Sep 1938	11 Aug 1940
7	Vol 9	12 Aug 1940	24 Sep 1940
8	scraps	4 Jun 1942	22 Jul 1943
9	Vol 10	16 Jun 1948	26 Jun 1950
10	Vol 11	26 Jun 1950	24 Nov 1951
11	Vol 12	25 Nov 1951	4 Jan 1953
12	Vol 13	4 Jan 1953	4 Jun 1954
13	Vol 14	28 Mar 1955	28 Oct 1956
14	Vol 15	20 Dec 1956	17 Nov 1957
15		15 May 1958	14 Mar 1959
16		8 Jun 1959	4 May 1960
17		6 Nov 1965	29 Aug 1966
18	scraps	3 Nov 1969	16 May 1970
19	scraps	29 May 1970	25 Feb 1971
20		7 Nov 1971	11 Aug 1972

Book	Volume	Start date	End date
21		19 Mar 1977	3 May 1978
22		1 Mar 1979	29 Sep 1979
23		30 Sep 1979	24 Jan 1981
24		21 Feb 1981	30 Aug 1981
25	scraps	14 Sep 1981	2 Sep 1982
26		24 Sep 1982	18 Aug 1983
27		25 May 1984	15 Apr 1985
28		3 May 1996	29 Sep 1996
29		28 Jun 1997	8 Apr 1998
30		13 Apr 1998	17 Dec 1998
31		19 Dec 2015	13 Sep 2016
32		12 Jan 2019	5 Sep 2019

The Rucksack Club of Queen's College, Dundee (now Dundee University), maintained visitors' books at Corrour Bothy from 1928 to the 1960s. Surviving books are housed in Dundee University Archives. In the late 1960s, the newly formed MBA took Corrour under its wing and since then provision of visitors' books has become erratic. Volumes have been left there by Nature Conservancy wardens, MBA maintenance officers and other individuals. Most of these are currently unaccounted for and may be held by a number of people or stored and forgotten about by one organisation or another. During research for this book, seven were found in storage at Scottish Natural Heritage in Aberdeen, two in the Scottish Mountaineering Club archives at the National Library of Scotland and one in individual hands. With the support of SNH, all but the SMC couple have now been moved to Dundee.

The Rucksack Club initially gave each book a volume number, but this became untenable as the years passed and was abandoned in 1958. Whether missing books have gone astray or simply never existed at all is an open question.

As well as large gaps in the historical record, there are smaller time gaps between consecutive visitors' books, often due to full ones not being replaced quickly enough. In the early volumes, there is sometimes an appeal on the first or last page to remove the book from the bothy and send it back to the Rucksack Club for replacement, but this is obviously (if necessarily) an inefficient procedure. Even if the full book reached Dundee, it would then take time to place a new one in situ, hence the gap in the timeline, for instance, from June 1954 to March 1955. The problem is highlighted by a minute of a club meeting of 1949: 'The visitors' book at Corrour Bothy having been full for some months (as far as known), it was decided that it should be replaced (by persons unspecified).'

For a variety of reasons, there may also be time gaps within a volume. Examples include pages torn out for kindling, nibbling by mice and general dilapidation. A Rucksack Club meeting of 1937 expressed concerns that Volume 6 'was disintegrating as a result of rough handling or damp quarters'. What remains of Volume 8 consists of no more than a few scraps of paper.

The problem of maintaining a visitors' book is not unique to Corrour. The growth of hillwalking as a leisure activity has seen a corresponding increase in the number of bothy visitors and, as a result, visitors' books fill increasingly rapidly. It is difficult for a voluntary charity such as the MBA to maintain them and archive them for every bothy within their remit. Apart from a few held in the MBA archive in the AK Bell Library in Perth (none for Corrour), the organisation currently does not consider visitors' books worth the considerable storage required to keep them. I hope this book shows this is a mistake, for Corrour at least.

Given the relative paucity of recent volumes, this book necessarily concentrates on the older volumes and the early years of Corrour's life as a bothy, but it is these that are in any case the most interesting to a modern audience. To fill gaps in the timeline and bring the story up to date, I have used other sources such as the Cairngorm Club Journal, the Scottish Mountaineering Club Journal, Rucksack Club meets books and press cuttings.

The first visitors' book was left in the bothy on June 27, 1928. The first page requests that all telegrams be sent to 'Comfort – Cairngorms' and notes that 'there's an excellent bar 9½ miles away'. This is Mar Lodge, now private but then open to the public. The Rucksack Club was still fond of the place during my time as a member in the 1960s. The bar was noted for its melt-in-the-mouth venison burgers and central log fire, both of which, when accompanied by the local ale, contributed to fondly remembered recuperative evenings after long days on the hill.

On the first page of the second visitors' book in 1929, concern is already being expressed about the condition of the bothy, with visitors being urged to keep it clean. It was to be a perennial problem.

In the 1920s and 1930s, the bothy was the hangout of hardy, mainly working-class, outdoorsmen, who would find their way to the Cairngorms by whatever means they could, including hitch-hiking. They would make long approach walks from all points of the compass, perhaps from Blair Atholl or Ballater, which could be reached by train.

They had to ford the Dee, which had no bridge. They had no Gore-Tex and often no sleeping bag. Instead, they slept on beds of heather in blankets or multiple layers of clothing. When even a cave was judged sufficient shelter, Corrour could seem luxurious by comparison. They found here free accommodation and a profusion of unclimbed routes that modern-day climbers can only envy.

They were mostly men. The Rucksack Club even had separate men's and women's sections. The former would hold meetings in the 'men's writing room', the latter in the 'women's swot room'. Minutes from a joint 1936 meeting tell of a 'long and lively discussion... wherein the merits and disadvantages of a mixed meet were carefully examined'. Although the men often frequented Corrour Bothy and left records of their visits, the women generally preferred to stay in lodging in Inverey or camp at Derry Lodge.

A graph of monthly visitor numbers at Corrour would show the expected annual bell-shaped curve, with many more visitors in the summer months than the winter months. Even in the early days, perhaps surprisingly, there were relatively few empty nights in summer. From November to February, except for Christmas and New Year, you were more likely to have the bothy to yourself.

This annual pattern has remained true throughout the bothy's history, although visitor numbers have greatly increased over the years. Today, especially in summer, you are even less likely to have the bothy to yourself. The MBA requests that parties contain no more than six members, but many travellers now choose to take a tent in case of overcrowding.

The 1940s see entries from soldiers going to war or seeking a few days' peace on leave in the Cairngorms. The lack of visitors' books for the years 1943–8 is unfortunate as it would cover the end of the Second World War and the return of soldiers to the range.

The 1950s welcomed a new breed of climbers and also an increasing number of young people from schools, from boys clubs (Boys Brigade, Scouts etc), from university climbing clubs, from Glenmore Lodge Outdoor Centre (opened in 1947) and on the Duke of Edinburgh (DOE) Awards scheme (founded in 1956). Among these were growing numbers of female visitors. In the surviving visitors' books, 1958 saw the first large group of girls arrive, when a party of nine girls and two instructors from Glenmore Lodge stayed overnight.

With improved transport and the building of a substantial bridge over the Dee in 1959, access to the bothy became easier and the number of day visitors increased substantially. From the visitors' books, it's often difficult to know who stayed the night and who was just passing through. The prime target of The Devil's Point directly above the bothy became a straightforward day walk from Linn of Dee.

More recent improvements have made the bothy more popular than ever. It was reconstructed in 2006. There are now toilets. The walk-in has been eased further by path improvements. Mountain bikers can cycle in to Derry Lodge and beyond. Cheaper foreign travel has encouraged more visitors from outside the UK, especially France, Germany and Holland.

As the bothy's popularity has increased, it has to be said that the literary merit of its visitors' books has not kept pace. There have always been entries of the 'Kilroy was here' variety, together with detailed descriptions of the weather and lists of bagged Munros written in an almost illegible scrawl, but the older books generally contain a higher percentage of more thoughtful and lyrical entries. Perhaps, when the bothy was harder to reach, it was more deeply appreciated, or perhaps its visitors were more committed and less blasé about the privilege of being in the wilderness. The 'spirit of the hills' was certainly much more in evidence then.

As the years have passed, writers have become much more likely to vent their views on topics that have no place in a bothy visitors' book, such as football teams, the Falklands War and Scottish independence. There's also more foul and abusive language. None of this is worthy of repeating and is fortunately in the minority. May that remain the case.

In the early books, we find a greater number of interesting entries, including romantic odes to Corrour, humorous asides, paeans to the Cairngorms and evocative drawings. One visitor agonises about going to war. Another is equally traumatised by being unable to ignite wet heather to summon up warmth. Another waxes lyrical on the pleasures of a sunset. In this book all of these are now given a public platform for the first time since they were penned (or, more likely, pencilled).

While the storm rages outside, the lone bothy writer will ponder the loneliness of the hills and the meaning of life. The communal bothy writer is more likely to indulge in sarcasm and wit at the expense of colleagues. If the weather is bad, he or she will write about the eeriness of the Lairig Ghru and the friendliness of Corrour. Good weather, on the other hand, affords an opportunity to complain about the mice and the untidiness of the bothy.

The visitors' books themselves vary in size from small pocket-books to exercise books and, in later years, larger and more substantial tomes. Many entries are difficult or impossible to read, even with forensic study, and not just because of degradation over the years. Ball-point pens did not become generally available until after the Second World War, so older entries are often written in long-faded pencil and without the greatest care, whether for legibility, spelling, punctuation or clarity. A 1951 entry describes dropping off a sharpened pencil at the bothy. How many visitors would think of doing that, or even providing a pencil sharpener? And how many visitor records have been lost because of the lack of a writing implement?

Dates of entries are imprecise, owing to multi-night stays or guesswork on the part of the writer. Much of the text, especially the signatures of the writers and their companions, is impossible to decipher. I have appended author names to entries whenever possible, but my apologies to others whose writings must remain uncredited to speak for themselves.

In the selection of entries that follows, I have edited extracts, corrected spelling mistakes and added punctuation where necessary to make them grammatically consistent and easier to read. With regard to place-names, for the most part I have retained the name as spelt, except for obvious spelling mistakes. Glen Einich, for instance, as it was known to generations of hillwalkers, has recently been Gallicised on Ordnance Survey maps as Gleann Eanaich. BEN MACDUI (in upper case), as named on current OS maps, was formerly named BEN MACDHUI and appears in the visitors' books under various guises (Ben McDhui, Beinn Mac Duibh etc). The correct Gaelic is Beinn MacDuibh.

Less than half a dozen entries are in Gaelic. Although early visitors were usually Scots, only a few are in the Scots language. Before the Second World War especially, there are more entries in Latin. The vast majority of entries are in English, even by visitors from abroad.

Of the many poems in the early books, some are reproductions of published works by poets such as Burns, Wordsworth, Shakespeare and Manley Hopkins. The Selkirk Grace appears several times, often misremembered. I haven't reproduced these here. Of the original poems composed in the bothy, some deserve a wider audience than a forgotten visitors' book. The older volumes also contain some well-drawn pictures, some of which are reproduced in this book.

To give shape to the chaos of entries, I have divided them into a number of themes, within which they are listed in roughly chronological order. Once you've read them, I hope you'll agree with one unknown, far-sighted person who wrote on the first page of Visitors' Book Volume 18 in 1971:

'Kindly do not remove or use for bumf or firelighters – this could be an historic document some day.'

A PERSONAL CONNECTION

I FIRST VISITED Corrour Bothy in 1965 as a wide-eyed bejant (first-year student) at Dundee University – then still a college of St Andrews University. At the Societies Fair in my first week, I joined the university's hillwalking club, called the Rucksack Club. Keen to explore the Highlands, I immediately volunteered to help out on one of the club's projects.

The club was involved in a survey of the semi-permanent snowbeds in Garbh Coire Mor at the head of Garbh Coire (see Page nn). Survey equipment had to be retrieved before winter storms set in and, on official business, we were permitted to drive the 3 miles from Linn of Dee to Derry Lodge. This was by far the easiest approach carrying heavy equipment. It was my first visit to the Cairngorms, but in truth I remember little of the trip except the wildness of the landscape. The sky was low, the mountains were decapitated, the light was dull and I was happy just to be involved, listening intently to the conversation of the older hands and storing away for future use every titbit of mountain-related information I could glean.

Despite the footbridge that had recently been built over the River Dee to ease access to Corrour Bothy, we bypassed it on the way to Garbh Coire and again on the way back. It seemed to me a stark, uninviting, ramshackle, stone building and I paid little attention to it. Ignorant of its history and purpose, I would never have dreamt of spending a night there. I was more preoccupied with the somewhat heavy equipment I had to shoulder back to Derry Lodge.

In the decades since, I have spent many days and nights in the Cairngorms and have become as fond of the old place as any lover of the backcountry. Far from the perimeter of the national park seen by the casual tourist, the interior is a hidden landscape that repays immersion in it, and Corrour is at its heart.

From the many times I have visited Corrour Bothy in the more-than-50 years since I first saw it, two memories stand out. On one frosty August night I was privileged to see the Aurora Borealis. Northwards over the Lairig Ghru, curtains of soft, rippling light reached out across the sky, silhouetting the peaks in such a way that you'd swear their outlines shimmered.

Even more deeply etched in memory is an April trip through the Lairig from Braemar to Aviemore in 1983. After hitching to Linn of Dee, my girlfriend and I walked to the bothy and camped overnight on a sheltered patch of low ground beside the Dee. On the following day, we set out to cross the summit of the pass, but the weather closed in and we found ourselves floundering in deep snow in blizzard conditions. Progress became impossible – at one point I walked into a vertical wall of snow that I couldn't even see when my face hit it. Completely disoriented, we had no option but to retreat.

As darkness closed in, we reached the bothy again, by now thoroughly exhausted, and tried to pitch the tent in the same spot as before. Without the heat generated by walking, our bodies lost heat fast. While my girlfriend dived inside for warmth, I struggled with frozen fingers to peg down the flysheet and stack snow around the hem for further stability. To no avail. No sooner had I dived inside myself, and removed boots to massage frozen toes, than the gale ripped the whole tent apart.

We would have been in a perilous situation had Corrour Bothy not come to our rescue. It was dirty, crowded and uncomfortable that night but, like many before us, never had we less cause for complaint. We spread the tattered remains of our tent down on the earth floor in a dank corner and snuggled gratefully into sleeping bags.

The following day, having shown us its worst, the Lairig gave of its best. In magnificent snow conditions, under a brilliant, brittle sky, we completed our journey to Aviemore through a wonderland of glistening fresh snow. Such is the magic of the Cairngorms.

In my first year at Dundee in 1965, I was so keen to explore the Highlands that I was the only person in the club to go on every meet, be it a day trip by hired coach or a weekend by car – in those days invariably belonging to a member of staff. It was often my responsibility to write details of ascents and climbs in the meets book, and it was as a result of this that I was asked in my second year to become editor of the Club Journal.

The journal was a small publication that appeared three times per year (once per term) and never ran to more than ten-or-so double-sided pages. In those pre-internet days, it was the organ by which the club disseminated information, opinions and other articles of interest. It contained a surprisingly wide range of topics for its time, including summer expeditions around the world (mostly written by staff members) as well as pieces on hills nearer home, how-to advice from senior club members and generally anything about which I could persuade any club member to put pen to paper (we had no word processors).

After the articles had been typed by the club secretary, I commandeered colleagues for an evening in the dedicated Rucksack Club room in the university's old Union building. There we made rough copies of the first page on a handle-operated Xerox photocopier and placed each page separately on a large table in the middle of the room. Then we copied and added the second page to the first to form the beginning of multiple piles. With each successive page the piles grew into complete journals.

Finally, we stapled each pile of pages together between bright yellow cardboard covers. The resulting literary masterpiece cost the princely sum of sixpence (2½p). These journals are now long forgotten, but I retain a small collection that I shall leave to Dundee University Archive if I ever fall off a mountain.

I would later become President of the club, passing on journal editorship to others, but it was in that second year, with the access to the club room that my position gave me, that I discovered the Corrour Bothy visitors' books and the club's involvement in their history.

The room contained little except a communal rope, odd bits of climbing equipment and a large tent to house those of us on weekend meets who had no tent of our own. There was also a dusty shelf that no one ever looked at. And on that dusty shelf leaned a number of dilapidated notebooks, their covers grubby, their spines broken or missing, their pages tattered and torn: the Corrour Bothy visitors' books.

The Rucksack Club was formed in 1923 and, with the bothy becoming an open refuge around the same time, it took on the task of maintaining a record of visitation. The first book was placed in the bothy in 1928 and here it was, along with others, in a little-visited back room at Dundee University.

As I leafed carefully through the disintegrating books, it occurred to me that these old records were of great historical interest to the story of Cairngorm hillwalking and climbing. Not that I was the first to realise this. The Rucksack Club even gave its approval for publication in 1952, although nothing came of it. Now, as editor of the journal, I could make some sort of amends, however minor.

Seeking to extract a selection of entries for publication, I studied the visitors' books in perhaps more detail than anyone had done before and published a few dozen 'Bothy Extracts' in an edition of the journal. I later revisited the resulting article for a chapter in my book *50 Shades of Hillwalking*, but there has been no concerted effort until now to revisit the source material itself and tell a more complete history of the bothy and its bothiers.

It is more than half a century since I first sat in the old Rucksack Club room and leafed through the visitors' books, but I'm pleased to say they still exist. No longer kept on a dusty shelf, though still rarely viewed, they now reside in sturdy boxes in the Dundee University Archive.

On my first research visit to the Archive, I was apprehensive about renewing my acquaintance with them. Could they still match my memory of them? Would they still be as evocative today as they were to that young wide-eyed student? I needn't have worried. The early books are now nearly a century old and, if anything, are more precious than ever.

When you see these venerable old books, now even more faded and ravaged by time, and hold them delicately in your hands, it's impossible not to be transported in imagination back to those early days of bothying. I'm at Corrour again. I experience again the howling gale, the swirling snow, the biting cold, the unforgiving floor, the warming fire, the conviviality of companions, the kindness of strangers and the irresistible pull of the wilds.

I hope I've done justice to all of the original authors who have made the visitors' books such a compelling read.

CORROUR THROUGH TIME

A HOME IN THE WILDERNESS

THE WATCHERS' BOTHY 1877–1920

CORROUR WAS ONE of several bothies built in the Cairngorms in the late 19th century to house a 'watcher' during the summer months. In those peak years of deer stalking on great sporting estates such as Mar, the watcher was a gamekeeper or seasonal employee whose job it was to report on deer movements and keep a lookout for poachers and other intruders, such as hillwalkers, who might interfere with the lucrative stalking business.

> Coire Odhar, or Corrour, is a famous resort of deer. In the ample bosom of the huge Corrour hollow, which rests at an elevation of about 200 to 300 feet above the river, there is abundant pasture. For ages the rich vegetable soil has been soaked with the dews of heaven, and the granite which forms the body of the mountain being near the surface, in July the place seems a paradise for frogs.
>
> Alexander Copeland, 'Cairn Toul and its Corries',
> CCJ No 16, 1901

There is no record of the bothy in the 1881 census and, in the Scottish Mountaineering Club Journal of 1893, Hugh Munro makes no mention of it in describing his walk through the Lairig Ghru. Similar descriptions of the pass in Cairngorm Club Journals of the time also make no reference to it. However, in the 1951 CCJ, George Taylor records visiting it in 1929, when 'the building was then 52 years old'. This gives a build date of 1877.

It definitely existed before 1883 because, as noted by Graham Ewen in CCJ No 101 (1988), there's a record of it being re-roofed in 1883. Perhaps, as he suggests, its absence from the 1881 census was because it was uninhabited at the time or it was just too remote for the enumerator to reach.

Its first mention in mountaineering literature comes in a potted guide to the Cairngorms, published in successive editions of the CCJ in the 1890s.

The Devil's Point is entitled to its designation. It is a great rocky pointed mass rising precipitously from the Lairig, to which it presents a seemingly inaccessible face. It may, however, be ascended from the Lairig along Allt a' Choire Odhar – there is a rough track for some distance – starting from a watcher's bothy known as Corrour.

Alex Inkson McConnochie, 'The Cairngorm Mountains III –
The Western Cairngorms',
CCJ No 7, 1896

Seven years later a similar article appeared in the SMCJ and this would later form the basis of the SMC's 1928 Cairngorms guidebook.

At the foot of the stream issuing from this corrie (*ie Coire Odhar*) is the 'Corrour' bothy, where the Dee may be crossed (if not in spate!).

WAS, 'The Western Cairngorms', SMCJ Vol 7, 1903

A succession of watchers occupied the bothy and, during the long, lonely summers in the Lairig, any passers-by were more likely to be welcomed than turned away.

This hospitable shelter, like the Hospice of St Bernard, has on occasion saved valuable lives, but is not always attainable. For, if the river is in flood, or Friar Tuck not in residence, the wayfarer has no chance of a venison patty or salmon steak for supper, with unlimited punch thereafter, and must trudge on by the Lairig to Aviemore or by Glen Luibeg and Glen Lui to Braemar. It is true the pasty and the salmon steak are imaginary so far as the writer's experience goes; yet true it is and of verity that he has vivid recollections of a wonderful tomato and macaroni soup served in the finest condition in this neighbourhood, with salmon from the Fraser River, beef *roti*, stewed prunes, and tea, coffee, and punch *ad libitum*. So profuse was the hospitality that in recrossing the river, wonderful to relate, he saw a double row of big stepping-stones where only a single row existed before meridian.

Alexander Copeland, 'Cairn Toul and its Corries',
CCJ No 16, 1901

At the turn of the 20th century, long-time occupant Charlie Robertson made an indelible impression on all who made his acquaintance. One of the last Gaelic speakers of the Braemar dialect, he was a fount of local knowledge who was said to know the hills better than anyone.

> To go over some of the map names with him was to discover the extraordinary number of inaccurate and distorted names which were put down by the first Ordnance Survey when mapping the Braemar district, a state of affairs which was not much remedied on the revised maps. From Robertson one could very frequently get a more correct name than that which appeared on the maps.
>
> Charlie Robertson's Obituary, CCJ No 75, 1934

Climbers often sought out his company and he would invite them in for a cup of tea with sugar and condensed milk, all of which he'd had to carry in himself.

> What happy memories I have of nights spent with him in the firelight – old Charlie in his big chair, and us squatting on the floor listening to his tales, with the wind shaking the little house and drawing sparks up the chimney.
>
> Hugh D Welsh, CCJ No 78, 1937

His legacy persisted long into the 20th century, such that when the Dee flooded in 1956 and carried a 19th-century frying pan down to Derry Lodge, local legend had it that this belonged to the man himself.

Another who made regular visits to Corrour in the 1900s, long before it became an open bothy, was the renowned naturalist and writer Seton Gordon (1886–1977), then still a young man learning his calling. He became friends with fellow piper John Macintosh, who succeeded Charlie Robertson as watcher, and often stayed with him. There's a famous photo of Seton sitting on the doorstep tuning his bagpipes.

> In those days Corrour had a box bed. The comfortable mattress for this was laid on the floor for the guest, who slept in the warmth of a fire of bog fir and peat. There were few climbers on the hills in those days and when I tuned my pipes outside the

bothy door the red deer used to approach and listen; they were
obviously excited by the stirring notes.

Seton Gordon, *Highland Summer*, 1971

The bothy often served as a B&B for Seton as he explored the
high tops in his kilt.

John Macintosh was adept at kindling a fire swiftly. However
early in the morning a start had to be made from the bothy, he
had the kettle boiling and a good breakfast ready. It was a cheery
wee room with its old box bed.

Seton Gordon, *The Highlands of Scotland*, 1951

When Macintosh wasn't in residence, he left the bothy locked.
During the week he'd be about his business on the hills. On a
Sunday, when there was no stalking, he'd invariably walk to his
Deeside home for the day. In winter, he stayed on Deeside. For
such times, he let Seton know where the key was.

[Arriving after midnight] We were able to locate the bothy only
by the murmur of the burn that flows down from Corrour (Coire
Odhar) close to the small building. We knew the hiding place of
the key, thanks to John Macintosh, and we groped our way into
the one small room and lit the candle set ready on the table. The
peat fire had to be coaxed into life, water fetched from the spring
and the kettle boiled. The bothy in those days was so clean that
we slept on a mattress on the floor. The wee room had a home-
ly and hospitable feeling such as no other I have lived in, either
before or since.

Seton Gordon, *The Highlands of Scotland*, 1951

On one occasion Seton holed up in Corrour during a Cairngorms blizzard of such ferocity that ptarmigans were sheltering
in his footprints in the snow. When his companion went out for
water, he had to guide him back with a blast on the pipes.

It was not until darkness fell and soon dispelled by the moon
that the storm was at its height. In the moonlight the Lairig was
almost as light as day. The snow had ceased to fall and overhead
stars could be seen but, across the ground and up to a height of
six feet or more, snow, white and solid as a blanket, was drifted
furiously by the frost-laden gale out of the north. We piled the fire

high with fuel but in that small room a basin of water, placed on
the table beside the window, eight feet from the fire, froze.

Seton Gordon, *The Highlands of Scotland*, 1951

Seton even attributed his Oxford degree in Natural Science to
his stays at the bothy as they enabled him to write a remarkably
authoritative answer to one of the exam questions: 'Write as fully
as possible what you know about the alpine flora of Britain.'

The last watcher at Corrour was Frank Scott. With improving
roads and motorised transport making access to the glens easier,
he left his station in 1920 and the building was abandoned by
the estate.

[Beyond the junction with the River Geldie] ...the majesty and
silence of the Cairngorms begin to cast upon us their irresistible
spell... Of human existence probably no sign will be seen save the
lonely Corrour Bothy far up the glen.

Rev George Walker, 'The Upper Dee in Summer',
Aberdeen Daily Journal, 1 September 1921

THE OPEN BOTHY 1921–49

ONCE THE BOTHY lost its custodian watcher, it wasn't long before the lock on the door was broken and walkers and climbers began to use the empty bothy as a refuge and base. One of the earliest references to its new calling comes in 1925 when the Cairngorm Club erected a mountain indicator at the summit of Ben Macdui. Well over 100 people came by various ascent routes for the unveiling ceremony.

> The Lairig also added its quota of, at least, one camping party, while the Corrour Bothy in Glen Dee – which in recent years appears to have attained the dignity of a climbing hut – contributed a quartet of ardent young spirits.
>
> Robert Clarke, 'Inauguration of the Ben MacDhui Indicator',
> CCJ No 64, 1926

The 'ardent young spirits' provided their own account in the press.

> When we set out from Corrour Bothy the valley of the Dee was quite clear and bright, but higher up the bluff shoulders of Ben Mac Dhui were lost in mist... Soon the sun pierced the pall of cloud, flooding the valley with light. It was a wonderful sight to see the climbers coming up to the unveiling. On a distant slope a dot, or group of dots appeared, and these slowly emerged as people and the crowd at the summit grew larger. By the time of the unveiling, 136 keen climbers, quite a few of them ladies, and some very youthful mountaineers, were grouped around the indicator for the short but very impressive ceremony. Now (*the summit*) has a neighbour consecrated to the task of guiding and informing the fortunate climbers and tourists who attain the Ben's lofty summit.
>
> RFS, 'Panoramic View of Scotland', *Dundee Courier*,
> 8 August 1925

A few years later, Corrour featured in the press in more tragic circumstances when it played a key role in one of the most demanding search operations ever undertaken in the Cairngorms. On 2 January 1928, Glasgow student Thomas Baird died after being found injured and unconscious near Gleann Eanaich Lower Bothy. In those days there were two bothies in Gleann Eanaich, both now long gone – a Lower beside the Beanaidh Bheag river and an Upper at the mouth of Loch Eanaich.

It was soon determined that Baird had not been alone and that his companion Hugh Barrie was missing. A search began. When no sign of the missing student was found in Gleann Eanaich, it was suggested that perhaps the pair had walked through the Lairig Ghru to Corrour and tried to cross to Gleann Eanaich from there. On 6 January a rescue party of six men set out from Derry Lodge, but conditions were atrocious.

> Progress was made as far as a point 400 yards east of Corrour Bothy but they could get no further. The snow was swirling into the men's eyes like fine sand, and blinding them. The journey from Derry Lodge to this point, a distance of less than five miles, had taken fully four hours. At the point where their path was blocked, they knew from local knowledge that the River Dee must be only 200 yards away. That river was completely out of sight under a covering of ice and snow. All of them were worn out, and on the journey back they encountered tremendous drifts of snow, and had frequently to push through these up to the armpits.
>
> 'Cairngorms Hold Their Secret', *Dundee Courier*,
> 7 January 1928

An Aviemore party was beaten back by the same blizzard, so on January 8 a larger Aviemore party of some 60 men set out to search the mountainsides above Gleann Eanaich. Again, there was no sign of the missing student, and some of the searchers themselves got into difficulty on the steep icy slopes.

In one of the worst storms in decades, another week passed before, on January 14, the Luibeg keeper and his son were able to reach Corrour. They found no sign of occupation, but two sets of frozen footprints led away from the bothy (see also Page 159).

It would be a month before the mystery was solved. Barrie's body was discovered in Gleann Eanaich, just a few hundred yards from the shelter of the Lower Bothy. Poignantly, he had written a piece for his university magazine the previous summer, which began 'When I am dead...'. It included the lines:

> But take my whitened bones far, far away
> Out of the hum and turmoil of the town.
> Find me a windswept boulder for a bier
> And on it lay me down.

In the same year as the tragedy, the Scottish Mountaineering Club's first guidebook to the Cairngorms was published.

> On the farther side of the Dee... is the Corrour Bothy, formerly occupied by a deer watcher in summer but now disused, and the best plan is to make for it.
>
> Henry Alexander, *The Cairngorms*, 1928

In June, Corrour acquired its first visitors' book and the recent tragedy may well have informed its first entry.

> O, haven of rest, may thy walls be blest
> With power to withstand for years and years
> The stormy wind that round thee tears
> And threatening doom.
> May thy door be open aye to those
> Who meet with mishap in the snows
> Or find themselves entrapped in throes
> Of deepest gloom.
>
> 'ALASDHAIR', 27 June 1928

A few years later, an anonymous author studied the first four books to produce a record of bothy usage. Such a task would now be impossible, not only owing to degradation of the material over the intervening years but also because Volume 4 is missing. The writer makes a number of unsubstantiated or exaggerated claims, eg nine out of ten local visitors to the Cairngorms visit Corrour, including a 'heavy proportion of lady climbers', but the approximate numbers remain of historical interest.

27 June 1928 – 12 Sep 1929 700
12 Sep 1929 – 12 Apr 1931   400
12 Apr 1931 – 19 Jun 1932 600
19 Jun 1932 – 7 Jul 1933   400

June and July are 'rush months' for climbers in the Cairngorms, and the entries in the books come thick and fast during this time, accounting for quite two-thirds of the entries. In August and September, they thin out rapidly and, during the five years covered by this novel census, only some 60 names were entered in the periods between October 1 and March 1.

...

Every year, with the spread of the tramping and climbing cult, these magnificent mountains become more and more popular. Yet it is only seven years since the writer lived in Corrour Bothy for the entire first fortnight of June – and saw only one other human being in that time!

A Mountaineer, 'A Census of Climbers',
Dundee Courier, 7 July 1933

By 1929, only one year after the Cairngorms tragedy, Corrour was being recommended in the press as a place to take a holiday.

Corrour Bothy is the ideal place to choose for your headquarters in climbing the Cairngorms... At first sight it is not at all inviting because of its dilapidated condition. Your first thought on entering is that you would rather sleep out in the heather, but at the end of another hour you find yourself enjoying a meal set on a table which is not quite up to dining room standards. In the day afterwards when you go out climbing you may find yourself giving a cheer when it comes into sight at the end of a long day's tramp.

'A Bothy Holiday in the Hills', Dundee Courier,
17 August 1929

The box bed described by Seton Gordon was still there in 1928.

The bed is not too bad when you've discovered the end where the head should rest – that and the adaption of one's anatomy to the mounds and dales of the mattress.

26 August 1928

But it didn't last out the year.

Arrived here 3.20pm after a 4 hours tramp in the snow. Found the
bothy in an abominable state, with the bunk smashed and mighty
little of the flooring left. Dug some roots out of the bog by the river
and got a good fire going.

                                                        1 January 1929

An old armchair that may well have been Charlie Robertson's
'big chair' appears to have lasted slightly longer.

I first visited Corrour Bothy, now the most widely known of all
Scottish mountain shelters, in 1929... I do recall vividly, amongst
some other fitments, a prodigious rough timber armchair in which
my companion and I were able to sit side by side. I observed also
a good deal of internal timber work, a partition, ceiling etc.
            George Taylor, 'The Reconstruction of Corrour Bothy',
                                              ccj No 87, 1950–1

The armchair made an impression on another visitor too, as he
recalled when revisiting Corrour years later.

Keeping old age at bay. Travelled by bus from Aviemore to
Braemar via the Lecht to attend the 'Gathering', as the games are
affectionately called by the Braemarians... I first came to the bothy in
1930. Then it was a cosy place, partitioned into two parts with over
a foot of heather on the floor. There was a stout wooden table. And
whadda ye think? A huge armchair.

                                                    4 September 1953

Dick Gowers, a leading light in the Creag Dhu mountaineering
club, also revisited in later years.

Many changes since my first visit in the 1930s – a loft to sleep in,
also an armchair, a food cupboard with large tins of sugar & tea, also
tons of food, no rubbish or tins left around the bothy, plenty of dry
heather to sleep on.

                            Dick Gowers, Creag Dhu, 1 October 1970

Before long the armchair was gone too, along with the partition,
the loft, the floorboards and anything else flammable. The heather
was necessary for insulation on the damp earth floor, especially in

the days before sleeping bags were in common usage. Visitors in those days were hardy folk, as recalled by Jock Nimlin.

> Aye, we were a bit harum-scarum, I suppose, delighting in caves where we slept wrapped up in newspapers like tramps, taking a pride in hard living, but being as comfortable as circumstances allowed. Not for us the kind of equipment that people take for granted today. These were weekends of simplicity I would not have missed.
>
> Jock Nimlin, reported in *Weir's Way*, 1981

Jock was another Creag Dhu man and pioneer Scottish mountaineer in the 1930s. Among other achievements, he founded the Ptarmigan Club and was later the first field officer of the National Trust for Scotland.

With no custodian, the bothy deteriorated so quickly that pleas to take better care of it were quick to appear in the visitors' books.

> Found the bothy without a table but ye gods what a mess. Is it necessary to tear up floorboards, bed boards etc to use as firewood? Need the cupboards be full of filth and littered with old bottles and candle grease?... Will future visitors kindly remember that to some the bothy is a hallowed spot and that the least —people can do is treat it decently and leave it decent.
>
> 17 May 1929

The second visitors' book even begins with an appeal to keep the bothy in good condition.

> Definition: A YAHOO is a person who makes use of the bothy and leaves it in a FILTHY CONDITION.
>
> September 1929

As is still the case today, such pleas made little difference to some.

> The mattress is now burning merrily in the ash heap and the seats – if any – and certainly the bugs are no more. Never has the place been so thoroughly scraped out and the good work must go on.
>
> 16 August 1931

There was even a poem addressed to the 'dismal Jimmies' who complained about the state of the bothy.

REPLY TO THE DISMAL JIMMIES

There's some wid need a store o' coal
Tae save then burnin' doon the bothy
An' some think this an awfu' hole
Dinna lauch – they need yer pity

There's some wid haul the place tae bits
An' lauch the while they're daein' it
An' ithers wid tak' purple fits
If they chanced tae be seein' it

There's some wid like a feather bed
An' some wid like hot water bottles
Ithers wid prefer instead
The kind ye empty doon yer throttles

There's some compleen the bothy's filthy
The micht set tee an' clean it
But none cam say it isna healthy
While there's a roof abune it

An' some with michty oaths impress
The lack o' comfort here among
But there will be a gey sicht less
Doon in yon place far they gang

An' fit think thee o' them, Corrour
Wi' a' their groans and lamentations?
Ye'll think they're a' sae muckle stour
That bore ye wi' their perorations.

E Rothney, 3 April 1932

When pioneer Scottish mountaineer, writer and photographer Ben Humble (1903–77) visited in the early 1930s, he nevertheless found the place a haven. After taking the train from Aberdeen to Ballater, he and a companion crossed Lochnagar to Inverey, where they spent the night at Maggie Gruer's (see Page 81). The following day they walked to Derry Lodge, collected a load of wood and carried it to the bothy.

> Corrour was indeed a haven. It is a small stone building, erected originally for a game watcher, but disused for many years... There is a big fireplace and heather for bedding. No one had been there since January, and the whole place was very damp. We were very glad of that load of wood and soon had a roaring fire going.
>
> Ben Humble, *On Scottish Hills*, 1946

In his later years, Ben was quite a character. With deafness giving his voice a raucous quality, he used to delight in shocking impressionable young Rucksack Club students with outrageous tales of his early exploits.

Another who found the bothy a welcoming refuge was one of the few female visitors to record an entry in the early visitors' books.

> My 'hubby' has often wished to bring me here and at last his wish has been realised through the kindness of his best friend who is with us now with his wife-to-be-I-hope. Our children Jim (aged 4 next Saturday) and Margaret (aged 1) are with their granny at Auchterarder. We are looking forward to bringing them some day with us – if it's still possible. We have found the bothy cupboard very well stocked and God bless the one who left the hatchet as we brought one with us and it broke into 'smithereens' (Woolworth's best steel, too).
>
> Mrs Greta Boyle, 2 October 1937

Syd Scroggie (1919–2006) also had fond memories of a 1930s visit.

> As I first visited it in 1938, Corrour was in a beautifully dilapidated state, just the thing to give a place character... There were one or two chairs, barely any longer in a condition to stand the weight of the deerstalker of old, but rickety and tied up with string; a table, dark with paraffin stains and scabby with wax, which seemed to lean up against the wall with the last of its strength; and in a corner to the right of the fireplace, a dirty old press (*cupboard*) with its door off the hinges.
>
> Syd Scroggie, *The Cairngorms Scene and Unseen*, 1989

Syd was 19 at the time. Five years later, near the end of the Second World War, he would lose a leg and his eyesight to a mine. That wouldn't stop him walking in the Highlands and writing poetry about them for decades afterwards. As he famously said, 'I can do without my eyes but I can't do without my mountains.' He returned to Corrour blind in 1955 (see Page 66).

The editor of the 1937 Cairngorm Club Journal ventured a more pragmatic view.

> The old bothy, once humorously referred to among its visitors as The Hotel, is now nearly a hovel. Its timbers have gradually disappeared as fuel, until little more than the roof remains. The gradual weathering of the roof and more rapid internal denudation must shortly bring the Corrour to the verge of ruin.
>
> 'Lui Beg', CCJ No 78, 1937

Alastair Borthwick (1913–2003), also visiting in the 1930s, was similarly more concerned with the practicalities of the accommodation than the romanticism of the setting. He reported recording an entry in Volume 6 of the visitors' books, although this doesn't exist in the surviving pages. In his classic book of reminiscences, he describes Corrour on approach from the north.

> Below [The Devil's Point], looking absurdly lonely, was Corrour Bothy. I saw people moving about inside it, so I left the track where a cairn marks the ford, waded the river and joined them. The bothy is no more than a small shed with an earth floor and a leaky roof; but there were six people living in it.... We fell to talking, sitting on biscuit tins in the middle of the floor.
>
> Alastair Borthwick, *Always a Little Further*, 1939

Pleas to treat the place with care continued.

Please keep this bothy tidy
And it will do its best
To shelter all the needy
When they come down to rest.

William W Cran, 23 July 1938

But vandalism was (and still is) so difficult to eradicate that rumours of demolition began to circulate.

Dear Sir, We have been told by a local climber that he had received news from a keeper that orders have been given to demolish Corrour Bothy in the near future. If your members have any plans for keeping Corrour we would like if you would communicate with our club as we use the bothy fairly regularly… and think that all members of the climbing and hiking game would give you their utmost support in any scheme

J Wyne, Creag Dhu, 27 July 1938

Rumours of demolition in the 1930s and 1940s were given substance by the bothy's increasingly parlous state and the demolition of bothies elsewhere, notably the two Gleann Eanaich bothies.

Arrived here in a very bad state from Aviemore, but the weather has been absolutely tropical since and has quite restored my youthful vim and vigour. I was very sorry to hear the Einich bothies had been demolished and I hope that the persons responsible for this vandalism meet their just repayment.

George Lamb, 20 July 1943

By the end of the Second World War, after over 70 years of withstanding Cairngorm storms, Corrour was beginning to come apart at the seams. The roof leaked, the door let in wind and the north gable was bulging outwards and close to collapse.

IT'S DULL, IT'S DANK,
IT'S WET, IT'S RANK,
IT LEAKS AT EVERY POINT,
BUT IT'S WEATHERED THE STORMS
IN THE HIGH CAIRNGORMS
AT THE FOOT OF THE DEVIL'S POINT.
(with apologies to Dangerous Dan McGrew)

Unsigned, on the first page of Volume 10 of the visitors' books, 1948

'The Shooting of Dan McGrew', referenced as inspiration for several bothy verses, was a well-known narrative poem by Robert Service.

Climbed Ben Macdhui via Tailors' Burn. Descended to Carn a' Mhaim
along ridge. Made hazardous descent over steep slabs to Corrour.

Four crumbling walls, a splintered door,
A leaking roof and an earthen floor,
This is the hole they call Corrour,
Where meat is high and milk goes sour,
Where midges, clegs and fleas abound,
And beetles crawl along the ground.

Patey, Rennie & Gibson, 3 July 1949

Tom Patey (1932–70) was 17 when he wrote this impression of
Corrour. He would go on to become the leading Scottish climber of
his generation and its most perceptive chronicler in prose and verse
(see Page 192). His first ascents were as wide-ranging as The Old
Man of Hoy sea stack in Orkney and the Muztagh Tower in the
Himalayas. He died when he fell while abseiling off The Maiden
sea stack in Sutherland.

ODE TO CORROUR

To the tune of 'The Mountains of Mourne'

Oh Dear Corrour Bothy's a wonderful sight
When you've climbed all day and you reach it at night.
You open the door and with eyes cast aloof
You gaze at the gaping great holes in the roof.
We've patched it with divots, we've patched it with tin,
We've worked all day long but the rain still comes in.
The walls they are cracking, the window's blown in,
There's a hole in the chimney where the wind whistles in.

The beds are made of heather all bounded by stones.
What a comforting feeling it has on the bones.
It must be admitted it makes a fine bed,
And there's nothing like granite for resting the head.
If you want a fire though you're tired as a dog,
You've got to go digging for wood in the bog,
And when you have cleaned it and dried it for days,
You'll find it will give you a wonderful blaze.

There's folks come in summer, especially in June,
And they find Corrour Bothy is really a boon.
It saves them from walking from Deeside to Spey,
Which is 28 miles, a long walk for one day.
So think of these things when at home or in pub,
Send thanks and donations to the Cairngorm Club.
They're sending up workers and *illegible* and tin,
And they're mending the roof so the rain won't come in.

WDW, 29 March 1950

The last verse hints at a major milestone in the bothy's history.

BOTHY RENOVATION 1950–2005

IN 1950, THE Cairngorm Club, with the cooperation of Mar Lodge Estate, undertook the task of renovating the bothy. The project leader was George Taylor, a club member and an engineering lecturer at Aberdeen University. His article, 'The Reconstruction of Corrour Bothy', in CCJ No 87 (1950–1) can be viewed on the club website: www.cairngormclub.org.uk.

The project was financed by an oversubscribed appeal and undertaken entirely by volunteers, not just club members but anyone who wished to help or happened to be passing.

> From all parts of Scotland – Glasgow and Edinburgh have been especially generous – and from as far afield as the South of England, donors have sent in money gifts large and small. The sum collected to date is in the region of £100. This will ensure a complete restoration of the bothy, which has given shelter to many hundreds of climbers, but which in recent years has fallen into serious decay, owing to lack of repairs.
>
> 'Corrour Bothy Will Be Restored', *Dundee Courier*,
> 11 February 1950

The main tasks were the replacement of the roof by aluminium sheets, the buttressing of the north gable and the installation of a new fireplace. The transportation of materials and equipment to the site was a huge task in itself. A helicopter was too expensive to hire. Wartime petrol rationing had just ended so a jeep could be used as far as the Luibeg Burn bridge, but beyond there everything had to be carried. Ponies were used on occasion, although manhandling them proved difficult – initially no one even knew how to saddle them.

An Aberdeen art student, SB Jolly, also volunteered to take 15cwt of cement and roofing felt to the bothy using a 30-horse-power

3½-ton wartime Bren-gun Carrier he owned. He drove while two assistants walked in front to point out obstacles. It turned into a five-day expedition, with the three-man party walking back to Inverey each night and returning to their task the following morning.

At one point, high on Sgor Mor above White Bridge, the carrier became stuck in peat and had to be unloaded in order to progress. The three men persevered until they got to within a mile of the bothy before dumping their load. The experience seemed not to faze them.

The first day of the climb was a bit rough,' Mr Jolly told a reporter of 'The Press and Journal, 'but I had done an assault course while I was in the Army, so I had an idea what these carriers could do.
'Students Take Cement up Cairngorms in Bren-gun Carrier',
Aberdeen Journal, 10 June 1950

For the most part, transportation was undertaken by a posse of helpers, often in rain described as 'incessant'.

I busied myself in quietly amassing and dumping in a multiplicity of peculiar places the heterogeneous mass of materials required: aluminium sheets, timber of various shapes and sizes and in an alarming quantity (from a transportation viewpoint) door, window, fireplace chimney can, cement, lime, steel bars, rolls of felt (*for insulation*) etc, and smaller stuff, though the porters may not have thought so, such as tools of all types, bolts, washers, nails, screws, door fittings, camping and cooking gear etc.

...

Some of the loads, such as the door, being heavy and indivisible, must have been a real heartbreak. Paradoxically, lightness was the problem with the large aluminium sheets. A strong wind threatened either levitation or decapitation. One completely disappeared, probably blown away.
George Taylor, 'The Reconstruction of Corrour Bothy',
CCJ No 87, 1951

Taylor and others recorded progress in the visitors' book.

June 27 The Lairig Club [*Aberdeen University*] transported the first consignment of roofing timber from Luibeg, under very showery weather conditions. It is hoped that more will follow. (Fiona K. Fraser)

July 8 Arrived last night and commenced, in filthy weather this
morning, pulling off the old roof and gutting the interior. The mouse
was definitely ejected from its nest in the base of the fireplace and
took refuge in a hole in the wall. (George Taylor)

July 10 1 ton of lime. Fell asleep en route... Have now erected
door, repaired fireplace and put up roof rafters. Everything appears to
be proceeding according to plan. (George Taylor)

On the following days, several trips were made to bring in
drums of cement and rolls of felt. Others brought in more food
for the workers.

July 11 Purlins [*horizontal beams*] nailed to rafters and some sarking
[*insulation*] and cementing done including lintel over door. Work quite
held up at 3pm by heavy rain. Most of us have gone to bed, hoping to
be more comfortable than during the night. Last night I had on three
pairs of trousers and three sweaters, one reversed as a fourth set of
trousers, and was still relatively miserable. (George Taylor)

July 14 Have been too busy (and hungry) to log our progress. Today
we concreted the bench at the window, finished reinforced lintels
over door and windows and commenced firing aluminium roof sheets.
Worked till 10.30pm. Weather very poor. (George Taylor)

July 17 I leave Corrour Bothy after 10 days of the hardest work I've
done in my born days. Mixed weather and leaking tent. (G. McKenzie)

July 20 Since the last entry, work has been proceeding steadily
in rather improved weather. Roof now completed and one coat of
Snowcem (*paint*) sprayed on the interior (and on ourselves) by stirrup
pump. A. Tewnion arrived on Sunday and has been building chimney
and buttress and painting the walls, working till 11pm. He is ably
assisted by our old friend R. Still of Luibeg Bridge fame. (George Taylor)

July 21 A very long day's work terminated with dinner at 12am.
Ceiling was fired and buttress completed. Work is nearing completion
and the two of us [*the other was Gordon McAndrew*] are spending
the first night in the renovated bothy after our tent was partially
burned by Cameron. A notable feature of our late dinner was fresh
strawberries brought via Ben Macdhui by Dr Stewart. (George Taylor)

July 22 The work of renovating this building has now been completed to the best of our ability. Much labour has been put into it by many climbers, known and unknown, and a large part of the materials has been donated by others. (George Taylor)

July 22 Leaving now after 16 days on the bothy, which now looks very good. It is to be hoped that future users of the bothy will not misuse it! As we leave it is raining – as usual. (G. McAndrew)

July 23 TODAY ENDS A FORTNIGHT'S VOLUNTARY HARD LABOUR. NOW FOR 50 WEEKS REST (AD Cameron)

George Taylor also constructed the original bridge over the Luibeg Burn in 1948 (see Page 89), built the Hutchison Hut in Coire Etchachan on Ben Macdui in 1954, undertook the reconstruction of Derry Lodge in 1955, rebuilt the Luibeg Bridge upriver in 1957 when the original was destroyed by floods, and in 1958 built bridges at Corrour, the Derry Dam and the Glas Allt. In 1964, he made one last nostalgic week-long trip into the Cairngorms to revisit Corrour and other sites before his health deteriorated. He died the following year.

Corrour Bothy was now, at least for the present, windproof and watertight, even if it remained a basic shelter with an earth floor. Visitors were impressed with the renovation, not only with the bothy's more welcoming interior, but also with the bright new aluminium roof that made it easier to find in poor light.

Arrived late from Braemar. New roof led us to bothy, which we would otherwise probably have missed in the dark. Appreciate greatly the hard work involved in making the repairs, which have made the place so comfortable.

H Barclay, 24 July 1950

Have spent two nights in the streamlined bothy – a great change since my first time here over 20 years ago. Congratulations to the builders – this time it's built to last.

J Douglas Beedie, 27 July 1950

Tonight there was quite a few wet and tired bodies arrived here from various directions. We spent a comfortable night

and are very grateful to the Cairngorm Club for such a
comfortable 'caravanserai'.

J Anderson, 30 July 1950

Speechless with admiration.

J Wilson, 16 August 1950

The bothy – a palace compared to 20 years ago.

AS Sullivan, 1 July 1952

There are many other entries equally grateful, notably the following, now faded, barely legible but epic eulogy:

SONNET ON THE TRANSFORMATION OF CORROUR

The pyramids of Egypt have stood sure
Non-changing monuments to human clay:
Long after present empires pass away
Those tombs of mighty kings will firm endure.
So shall the wondrous phoenix of Corrour
Preserve this memory from time's decay
Who laboured here like Hercules, that they
And future wanderers might rest secure.
All honour to their unrecorded names!
In fortune's favour may their days be set
And they ne'er worse roof find than this they made.
Their selfless toil most grateful homage claims
From all who love these hills. O, huge our debt,
By careful tenancy alone repaid.

Denis Butler, 25 May 1951

A few visitors bemoaned the changes made to the old place. Syd
Scroggie was one. Having lost his sight during the war, he returned
to Corrour blind in 1955.

> Gone were the table and chairs, loft ladder and press. There was
> now no flooring at all, not even the mutilated planks and joints
> you tripped over of old; only beaten, bare peat soil, relieved along
> the back wall by plucked heather laid down for bedding.

The old tarry roof had been redone in gleaming sheet aluminium. There was a kind of cooking-bench in rough concrete on the same wall as the door; and the door itself, solid and true, was in striking contrast to the creaky, friendly, old wreck we remembered.

...

Now the bothy had a more clinical air, as if the planners had moved in, and though it was obviously wind and weather tight, and would remain so for decades, it had lost much of its character in the process. The body of Corrour had risen from the grave into which it had virtually collapsed during the War, but it had become disassociated from the soul we remembered.

Syd Scroggie, *The Cairngorms Scene and Unseen*, 1989

In the years to come, others would suggest further improvements.

Her first visit, and suggests carpets would be an improvement.

Norma Gourlay, 5 August 1955

Great day to do the Lairig Ghru. Totally surprised by the excellent facilities the bothy offered – bar, disco – amazing.
Yes – well amazing what hypothermia does to the mind.

Marion Mackinnon, 3 August 1996

Could do with some nice floral print wallpaper and a bowl of pot Pourri, but apart from that a very pleasant evening.

Steve and Gary, 28 September 1996

I think your bothy is rather nice but could do with a nice splash of colour paint and maybe a small toilet for us girls.

25 May 1998

Weather terrible but company and accommodation reasonable. Could do with bath facilities etc.

Louis Forno, 18 July 1998

One feature the planners did not touch was the growing rubbish dump.

We did not clear the rubbish dump; some of my companions
protested that it would be almost sacrilege to remove the heap of
tins, one of the famous features of the Cairngorms.

George Taylor, 'The Reconstruction of Corrour Bothy,
ccj No 87, 1951

Of course, there were some who were too lazy even to use
the dump.

Do the above party think the interior of the bothy & the fireplace in
particular is a rubbish dump? In future they may have the energy to
throw their leavings as far as the dump 20 yards from the door.

11 April 1950

So many people have been complaining about the unsightliness of
the surroundings without, be it noted, doing anything about it, that
this morning, before leaving, Doreen collected all the old papers
around and burned them. Also collected many tins then threw them
on the rubbish dump. If everyone who comes here and thinks the
place untidy does the same, then very soon the only unsightly thing
will be the dump itself. That will need a small gang to hide it, and
another to dig a second pit.

Alex Tewnion and A Doreen Tewnion, 30 July 1955

Alex (Sandy) Tewnion had helped in the 1950 renovation of the
bothy and visited it many times (see Page 195).

The dedicated rubbish dump helped to keep the bothy and its
surroundings clean and tidy, but over time it, too, would become
an environmental hazard.

Following the bothy's renovation, the visitors' books were soon
back to recording normal comings and goings in the Lairig Ghru.

Pause, stranger, softly shed a tear
On August the ninth thirteen slept here
The house simply could not hold more
Unless someone slept outside the door
But the bed was dry, the company good
The wind outside we quite withstood.

J Gaskin, 9 August 1955

Last night there were 12. Tonight there will be 22 if we stay, so we make 20 by moving on [having a tent]. The bothy will be worn out soon!

Glyn Jones, 3 July 1956

The building of the 1959 bridge over the Dee opposite the bothy (see Page 101) made it even more popular. In the late 1960s, the newly formed MBA took over maintenance of the building and, from then on, regular working parties buried rubbish and gave the place 'a good clean out'.

Surviving visitors' books from the 1960s are few and far between. The following letter written to the Rucksack Club in 1958 illustrates how easily they can be lost.

> My companion and I left the bothy on the 30th November '57, taking the completed book with us. It was our intention to post it… but we didn't because a mile from Derry Lodge we met a climber who offered to return the book for us, and we handed it over. I cannot give you the person's name but here are a few other facts which may help you in tracing him…
>
> Letter to Rucksack Club by JW Docherty, 4 April 1958

That particular visitors' book eventually did find its way back to the Rucksack Club, but many others remain missing, including that for 1961, when an attempt was made to replace the lost wooden floor.

> I first stayed here in 1961, when a party of us decided to renovate the bothy. We put in another wooden floor and panelled the walls, rather than using planks. We brought in all the materials using garrons [ponies] kindly lent to us by Mar Lodge Estate. Unfortunately, the next time we visited in 1964 all the panelling and the floor had ended up the chimney once again.
>
> Colin Campbell in a letter to Neil Reid

In 1966, Robin Campbell, then editor of the SMC Journal, compared Corrour with the Sinclair Hut on the other side of the summit of the Lairig.

> Between these two it is a real Hobson's Choice with Corrour the winner by a short lump of dung. Both are completely lacking

in comfort of any kind. Both boast perennially wet and muddy floors, poor insulation and no fires. There is a fireplace at Corrour but any attempt to light it is frustrated, as we proved to our satisfaction in 1964.

Robin N Campbell, 'Birchermuesli, Braeriach and Blunders',
SMCJ No 157, 1966

It was around this time that the MBA took the bothy under its wing.

Stone Cottage. In need of good lime or whitewash inside and ditto outside in a suitable blending colour. One room with earth floor. Doors and windows are in good order. The only furniture is a stone table and stone shelf. There is a housebook (visitors' book) but no first aid kit. Water from the burn 20 yards away... No outbuildings. Only bog pine and heather for fuel, but there is a fireplace. No tools. Will sleep 10 in comfort.

Field Officer's Survey, 9 July 1967

The stone [cement] table, built during the 1950 renovation, had an indentation that collected all kinds of debris. By the 1960s, it was said that you only had to pour hot water into it to obtain a nourishing soup.

Despite the work done in 1950, the earth floor was as it had always been and its regular dampness was a continuing source of complaint. The main problem was that water seeped in from the slopes of The Devil's Point above. In 1968, the dampness problem became the focus of heated MBA discussions. What to do about it? Some wanted to cement the floor while others didn't. Even the bothy's field officer was unsure.

It is unnecessary to cement the floor when there are so many other vital work projects needing doing. There is no visitors' book – an urgent requirement, I suggest.

Field Officer's Survey, 21 April 1968

Cement was in fact carried to Corrour but for various reasons, including the influence of the 'anti-cement' faction, the difficulty of organising working parties and the urgency of more vital projects on other bothies, it was never used. Instead, nine inches of soil were dug out of the bothy floor to reach gravel then heavy polythene bags were laid down, topped with clean soil and finally dry peat fibre. However, there was still seepage and it was agreed that the job was much bigger than anticipated.

A 1972 field officer's report spelt out the problem.

> Floor lower than surrounding ground, needs raising 1ft. But if raised, rising damp problem. Even if concreted, needs a waterproof membrane. Drainage ditch behind bothy considered, but again a large job [according to calculations, it would have to be 4ft deep].
>
> Field Officer's Survey, 1 October 1972

The following year's MBA report indicates that an attempt had in fact been made on a ditch.

> Clean, but draught under door only excluded by cutting of well-fitting sod! Emergency food/fuel pan non-existent, but perhaps it would be stolen. Mouse. Well-dug trench at rear should help drain water.
>
> Field Officer's Survey, 30 August 1973

At some point in the 1980s, the floor was finally concreted over. The litter problem, however, remained unsolved, to such an extent that it was even highlighted in a book on the area's natural history and scenery.

> There are big heaps at Corrour and a pile several feet high inside Curran hut on the plateau.
>
> Desmond Nethersole-Thompson and Adam Watson,
> *The Cairngorms*, 1974

With the growth of hillwalking as a leisure activity, overcrowding was also becoming a more regular problem.

> Had planned to stop here tonight after a long tiring day but found no room at the inn. Can't say we approve of large parties ensconcing themselves in the only suitable shelter hereabouts to the exclusion of others.
>
> MBA member, 2 July 1980

This complaint incurred the following reply.

> Last night 7 of our party (of 14) slept in this bothy – hardly excessive in a place this size. Parties like ours are dictated by the economics of

minibus size – bigger than I'd like, but there it is. We carry tents but use bothies like these too, for the same reasons as everybody else does – to reduce backpacks (in this case carried by schoolchildren). We slept in the bothy last night because the weather was foul and there was only one other occupant.

3 July 1980

Cleanliness similarly continued to be a problem.

This is a lovely book. It's a pity it's wasted on people writing so much rubbish. Also <u>leaving</u> so much rubbish, which I have had to dispose of and carry out with me (as part of my job for the MBA).

Margaret Pryde (MBA), 3 August 1996

Another (anonymous) MBA member did sterling work the following summer.

Walked in from Derry Lodge to clean up the bothy and surrounding area. Filled 19 large canvas mail bags and burned as much again. If this rubbish problem continues the estate could take drastic actions.

19 August 1997

By the following summer, the bothy was back to its usual state.

Not very amused at the amount of rubbish that has been left so come on lads, do your bit and carry everything away with you (this includes the five pairs of sweaty socks I have just cremated!). If an old 59-year-old female with spectacles can do it, <u>so can you</u>. Have cleaned the place and left it tidy as always. All the best.

Margaret Pryde (MBA), 15 September 1998

Margaret's work did not go unappreciated, as recorded by a visitor three days later.

The bothy was clean and will hopefully stay that way. If I had a hat I would take it off to all of the caring souls who keep mountain refuges this way. They are a godsend. And to those who say a hut should be closed down owing to an accumulation of rubbish left by the uncaring few, I pose a question: if this hut were not here, where do you think the uncaring few would dispose of their rubbish? I suspect in the hills around. So do not punish the many, who respect and contribute to the glories of this

nature, by closing or threatening to close this refuge hut. Rather educate
and promote the sensible practices of Recycling, Reduction and Re-use.

Paul Walker, Earthwalker, Earthman, lover of this planet, on a 3,500 mile 'Walk for
Freedom' and a much larger Fairytale Journey through Life, 18 September 1998

As Corrour entered the third millennium, its 1950 renovation
by the Cairngorm Club was 50 years old. The building was once
again beginning to succumb to wear and tear. Again, something
needed to be done.

BOTHY RENOVATION 2006–present

IN 2006, THE MBA devoted a large slice of its funds to a more complete renovation of the bothy than had ever been attempted before. Even the planning was much more difficult than in 1950. The estate was now owned by the National Trust for Scotland, it lay within a Site of Special Scientific Interest and, since 2003, within a national park. A long bureaucratic delay ensued while the various bodies ensured that all the necessary regulations were adhered to.

MBA accounts show that £7,607 was spent on the project in 2006, plus more the following year. It would have been even more expensive, but insulating material left over from the recent re-build of Bob Scott's bothy near Derry Lodge, following a 2003 fire that burnt it down, helped keep costs under control.

A substantial sum went on a helicopter to transport the bulk of the materials, including a generator, but it was still a mammoth undertaking. The vehicle track from Derry Lodge to the Luibeg Burn had been rewilded by the NTS in the 2000s, so even more footslogging was required beyond there than in the 1950 reconstruction.

The project was overseen by Kenny Freeman and most of the work was completed by the end of September 2006. Work undertaken included:

Replacement of front door

Installation of wooden floor, ceiling and wall lining, insulated with sheep's wool

Addition of an inner storm porch with door

Addition of a sleeping platform for two, with room underneath for another two

Fitting of a new multi-fuel stove with a new flue

Addition of a toilet extension

74

46 different people made a joint total of 113 trips over 18 working weekends, notching up 1,808 miles of walking in the process.
Neil Reid, 'Renovating Corrour', CCJ No 109, 2011

There are unfortunately no visitors' books for this period.

As in 1950, the weather wreaked havoc. The 1950 roof panels were still in a good enough state to be left in place, but the new roof sheets for the toilet extension again proved unwieldy in wind and again nearly resulted in decapitation of the project leader.

> The sheet that flew at Kenny was my fault. I had removed the stones holding the pile of sheets down, about to lift a sheet. Someone called me to do something and I turned away without replacing the boulder on the roofing sheets – and seconds later a gust lifted the top one and it flew through the air. Kenny put an arm up to deflect it and avoided disaster.
> as told by Neil Reid

Rain again arrived at the wrong time and, when it didn't, there were other annoyances.

> Passing walkers must have thought they'd come on the James gang hideout, with us all masked up to try and deter several millions of incredibly persistent midges.
> Neil Reid, 'Renovating Corrour', CCJ No 109, 2011

Again, as in 1950, the whole operation proceeded with a good deal of partying amongst the hard work. Most of the workers met up in Bob Scott's bothy on a Friday night, but on a Saturday Corrour often witnessed 'serious ceilidhing until half-past collapse o'clock'.

> [They were] nights that epitomised what bothy culture is all about. Where else do you find groups of folk, from 10-year-olds to over-70s, from all walks of life and all corners of the globe, pitching in together, sharing songs and experiences, food and even dry clothes on occasion.
> Neil Reid, 'Renovating Corrour', CCJ No 109, 2011

The most revolutionary improvement was the experimental VIP toilet. This was not, as its name might imply, for the benefit of visiting celebrities. It was a 'trial toilet based on the Ventilation-Improved

Privy with modification and adoption of the de-watering bag system... using geo-textile bags draining to a soak-away' (a 10m trench). There was some debate about whether the toilet should be tried in a less environmentally sensitive spot first, but in the event installation went ahead. It was originally intended to be located some distance away from the bothy, but instead it was incorporated into a bothy extension (which at least avoids a trek on a stormy night).

In the years since the toilet was installed, bags of solid waste have been changed regularly by maintenance organisers Neil Findlay and Neil Reid, with a changing but dedicated team of volunteers dressed in white boiler suits and rubber gloves – Corrour's very own forensics team.

It was originally hoped that the waste would compost sufficiently to be scattered over the ground, but the temperature in the Lairig Ghru prevents it from breaking down quickly enough. Instead, full bags are stored in a locked storage room and intermittently removed either by tracked vehicle or helicopter, eventually to a treatment facility in Aberdeen.

In 2009, the MBA decided, for the first time, to publish a list of all its bothies, including Corrour. Not everyone agreed with this policy, which may well have encouraged even more visitors, but a 2007 memo by MBA General Secretary Peter King records why it was considered necessary:

(1) To encourage more bothy users to support maintenance and to contribute by volunteering their time.
(2) To combat unauthorised lists such as those appearing on the web.
(3) To foster the organisation's charitable status, awarded in 1975. (Because a criterion for charitable status is 'public benefit', continued secrecy might become a problem in the future.)

That's not the end of the story, because ongoing maintenance will always be required of a public building in such an inclement environment. There have also been a couple of major developments at Corrour since 2006. By 2014, the multi-fuel stove was showing signs of wear and tear and was replaced by a more efficient fireplace and, in 2018, more substantial changes were made to the toilet annexe.

The toilet was such a success that the waste bags filled up more quickly than anticipated. In the summer months, MBA volunteers had to trek into the Lairig every month to change them. In 2018, to halve the number of visits required, the interior of the toilet extension was revamped to increase capacity from two seats (of which only one was in use at any one time) to four seats (of which only two are in use at any one time).

The visitors' books are full of praise for the MBA's provision of a toilet in the wilderness.

Thank you, MBA. Best lav in the world and lovely bothy.
Caroline & Nick, 23 May 2019

But abuse of the bothy by inconsiderate visitors still remains a problem. Although the former rubbish dump, which became such an eyesore and environmental hazard, has been removed, there are still those who seem incapable of following the 'Pack it in – pack it out' principle. Burning or removal of rubbish, abandoned kit and food remains a recurrent MBA maintenance task. Even worse, within a week of the new toilet annexe being opened, it was vandalised by a group of people who camped outside and held a drunken late-night party in it.

Such selfishness not only ruins the bothy experience for others but could have more serious consequences. One of Corrour's ongoing functions is to provide shelter in an emergency, as evidenced by continuing mountain rescue call-outs, sometimes requiring helicopter air-lift of injured or distressed parties from the bothy. In April 2019, for instance, three exhausted Polish walkers were rescued from Corrour (see Page 204). In July of the same year the possible consequences of anti-social behaviour were highlighted by an even more serious incident at another bothy.

Scotland's bothies are increasingly being used as rowdy party dens. There have been reports of vandalism and fires, and in one dangerous case of antisocial behaviour a group of hillwalkers had to be rescued after they were refused access to a remote shelter by revellers and were left outside in the cold and dark.
Douglas Barrie, *Scottish Daily Mail*, 10 July 2019

The MBA position remains that bothies must be open to all and not just available to those who know their secret locations, but the latest outrages have reignited debate in the hillwalking community about the promotion of these locations, not only online and in books, but also in walking magazines and television documentaries.

Following the 2019 incident, Police Scotland launched Bothy Watch – a multi-agency initiative involving the MBA, Forestry and Land Scotland, local authorities, mountain rescue teams and others – with the aim of carrying out regular checks on bothies and monitoring vehicles parked in certain areas.

> Nowadays there is a wealth of information available online about their locations and as a result they have become generally more accessible. This trend for the bothy has attracted a different type of user and we are concerned that health and safety on the hills is compromised and the integrity of the bothy lost.
>
> PC Samantha Briggs, Bothy Watch leader, 9 July 2019

At the time of writing, the initiative applies only to 11 MBA bothies in the south of Scotland. A more remote bothy such as Corrour is more difficult to monitor, but bothies are not law-free zones and responsible visitors should be aware of how to report vandalism and anti-social behaviour.

(1) Use the Report section of the MBA website.
(2) Phone Police Scotland on 101 (999 for emergency calls).
(3) Phone Crimestoppers on 0800 555 111, where anonymity can be maintained.

The use of the term 'a different type of user' is telling. Unsociable behaviour fuelled by alcohol is becoming an all-too common occurrence in a number of Scottish rural locations, not just in bothies. Drunken disturbances have already necessitated the banning of popular wild camping spots on the shores of Loch Lomond and is a problem in accessible glens elsewhere. Beaches such as Portobello and Troon have also become plagued by aggressive gatherings. At Troon in 2019, police used drones with on-board cameras for the first time to crack down on one such incident.

It is to be hoped that similar technology, with all the concerns it raises, will not be required to ensure the integrity of remote bothies.

Meanwhile, the position at Corrour remains as it has always been: we can only applaud the sterling work done by the MBA volunteers who maintain it... and hope that the moronic minority do not ruin bothying for the responsible majority.

In this respect, a press piece from over 80 years ago is worth repeating:

> In the Cairngorms a party of young Frenchmen discovered that Corrour Bothy, the only human habitation in the long traverse of the mountains, had been wilfully despoiled, and the famous Shelter Stone, where countless hundreds of climbers have found haven, left in an indescribably filthy condition.
>
> ...
>
> The Cairngorm outrage is not only vandalism; it is downright wickedness. The stone and the bothy are the only shelter in a wilderness of mountain, and to them in times of storm many mountaineers have owed their lives. To end the usefulness of such refuges may some day be found morally to be nothing less than murder.
>
> ...
>
> We need just one or two people of this brand to bring disrepute on hundreds and thousands of thoughtful and considerate men and women. That is why the outrages of the vandal reflect on every one of us, and why we must oppose him with every means at our disposal.
>
> RAD, 'Vandals Spoiling Scotland', *Dundee Courier*,
> 27 August 1936

GETTING THERE
EARLY APPROACHES

TODAY WE TAKE for granted easy road access to the main starting points for the walk-in to Corrour – the Aviemore area in the north and Linn of Dee near Braemar in the south. This wasn't always the case. In the early days of Corrour's life as a bothy, roads were rough, cars were few and buses were expensive to hire even for a mountaineering club. Access was easier by rail.

The Highland Railway, linking Perth to Aviemore via Drumochter Pass, was opened in 1863 and extended to Inverness in 1898, easing access from both north and south to Aviemore and the western fringes of the Cairngorms. From Aberdeen to the east, the quickest way to reach Corrour was to take the Inverness line (also opened in 1863) to Craigellachie then change onto the Speyside Railway (1863–1968) to Boat of Garten and Aviemore.

> In those days a wonderful excursion train left Aberdeen each Wednesday at one o'clock in the afternoon, ran to Aviemore, returning the same night, the first class return fare half a crown [12½p]... The afternoon excursion to Strathspey from Aberdeen was really a remarkable achievement. The first stop was Craigellachie, 68 miles from Aberdeen and was reached in 85 minutes – a much slower journey at present.
>
> Seton Gordon, 'The Highlands of Scotland', 1951

An alternative approach from Aberdeen was to take the Deeside railway (1866–1966) to Ballater, 17 miles from Braemar. This was the approach used by Ben Humble and others in the 1930s (see Page 56). From Ballater, it was a two-day walk to Corrour, with an overnight stop somewhere along the way. Some walked over Lochnagar, others took a more direct route along the north or south Deeside roads. Until the closure of the Balmoral section for Queen Victoria's Highland retreat in 1959, it was possible to walk all the way along the south side of the Dee to Braemar. With luck, you might even get a lift from the local postie on his mail-gig – a horse-drawn carriage.

> It was in lovely July weather that the forenoon train set us down at the familiar little terminus at the foot of Craigendarroch... Our preliminary spin was from Ballater to Inverey – a fairly effectual leg-stretcher. But then we had all that travellers could desire high spirits, good weather, Highland air and congenial company... To anyone in love with Nature the south Deeside road offers absorbing titbits at every step.
>
> William Skea, 'Ballater to Lynwilg', CCJ No 17, 1901

Maggie Gruer's Thistle Cottage boarding house in Inverey, close to Linn of Dee, was a popular haunt.

> For 50 years Maggie welcomed walkers, cyclists, climbers and tourists from all over Britain. Never during all that time did she turn a wanderer from her door. At all hours of the day and night they came. Many spent a night in that cottage before facing the adventure of crossing the Lairig Ghru, or made it a base for climbing Ben Macdhui or Cairntoul or for visiting the Shelter Stone.
>
> Ben Humble, *On Scottish Hills*, 1946

Her scones were famous, as recorded in her visitors' book.

> If I perish in the Pass
> At least I'll perish knowing
> That when I died I had inside
> The nicest breakfast going.
>
> Ben Humble, *On Scottish Hills*, 1946

So fondly was she remembered that her passing in 1939 merited a tribute in the Scottish Mountaineering Club journal.

> Her couthie fireside was the resting-place after many a hard day on the hills. Her quaint bedrooms and sleeping neuks could be as welcome as any Ritz bedroom to the bedraggled 'laddies' down from the Shelter Stone or from Corrour.
>
> ...

To climbers Miss Gruer's great gift was her uncanny appreciation of their wants and weaknesses. This was understandable, for they had been her life.

EWS, CCJ No 80, 1939

From Dundee and other points south the most popular approach to Corrour was to take the Inverness train to Blair Atholl and walk in from there over one or two days.

There are two favourite ways of going to it from Dundee. One way is to go via Braemar, Linn of Dee and Derry Lodge, or via Blair Atholl, Glen Tilt, Bynack Lodge and White Bridge... From Blair Atholl to Corrour is between 25 and 28 miles, and it is a whole day's work (12 to 15 hours) for most people to get themselves and their packs from the one place to the other.

'A Bothy Holiday in the Hills', *Dundee Courier*, 17 August 1929

It was a long walk, but early bothiers were nothing if not hardy.

We could keep up a four-miles-an-hour gait for hour after hour. We carried no tents and some of us carried no blankets or sleeping bags. It hardly seemed worthwhile, as we had so little time for sleep. Nowadays, when I cover some of these routes by car, I am astonished at some of the huge distances we walked just to get to the hills.

Jock Nimlin, reported in *Weir's Way*, 1981

More often than not, if only because of the railway timetable, it would be a two-day walk from Blair Atholl to Corrour, with an overnight stop in the vicinity of Bynack Lodge. Lodging en route could be found at Forest Lodge in Glen Tilt (NN 932741), at Bynack Lodge (NO 000855) over the watershed or at other remote dwellings, and camping or sleeping in outbuildings was always possible. Near Bynack, a pony hut served as a primitive refuge until the 2000s, when it was blown down in a storm and removed.

In 1924, a party of eight Rucksack Club members left Dundee for a winter meet at Corrour.

This fairly large party detrained at Blair Atholl in the small hours of the morning, bound for Corrour. The night was very dark, a slight mist was falling, intensifying the quietness of the night, and it was with a feeling of adventure that we stealthily opened the lodge gate and stole through the beautiful grounds of the Duke of Atholl with the River Tilt raging beneath.

Proceeding rather slowly, Forest Lodge was reached just before dawn and thereafter the procession up the glen widened until wide intervals separated the different groups. All arrived safely at Bynack. However, Mr Fleming, on his first time up, missed the lodge and walked on to the shepherd's hut a mile and a half further, where after getting some tea he was sent back.

As Mr Fraser wished to reach Aviemore next day, he and Mr Milne resolved to carry on up Glen Dee to Corrour that night – a rather hazardous undertaking without lanterns. It was growing dark when they left Bynack. The going was easy from Bynack to White Bridge, after which it was impossible to see a yard in front of you. In an endeavour to locate the path they climbed away from the river, where the going was more difficult. Falls were frequent and on one of them Mr Milne split open his forehead.

Eventually Corrour was reached at 1am in the morning. The journey of about eight miles from Bynack had taken nine hours. Both men were dead tired, having been on the road for 22 hours with heavy packs and a rope, and having partaken of only one meal since they left Dundee two nights before.

Luckily the bothy, which had taken a good deal of finding in the unfamiliar light, was occupied by two other members of the club, who had arrived the day before from Aberdeen... A good night's sleep worked wonders.

A Neil Milne, Rucksack Club meet report, December 1924

The following day Mr Fleming continued through the Lairig Ghru to Aviemore, the rest of the party arrived and a few good days walking on surprisingly snow-free mountains was had by all. Some then returned through Glen Tilt to join the train at Blair Atholl while others walked through the Lairig Ghru to board at Aviemore.

Five years later, despite an inauspicious start, another Rucksack Club party had a similarly rewarding trip from Blair Atholl.

The party detrained at Blair Atholl at 3am and set off up Glen
Tilt. Shortly after the start, however, heavy rain came on, accompanied by a strong head wind. At Forest Lodge the party was well
received and given the use of a fire. As the rain and wind continued, and one of the party was not feeling well, it was decided
to spend the night there. This meant two days were occupied in
reaching Corrour.

...

Most of the neighbouring peaks were climbed in glorious weather,
the snow being in very good condition.

HI Morris, Rucksack Club meet report, March 1929

The party split to return to Dundee, some via the Lairig to
Aviemore, others by a long tramp via Ballater and Glen Muick
to the station at Kirriemuir (see below). Forest Lodge is now a
private lodge reached by a private Land Rover track up Glen Tilt.

Another popular route was from Straloch on the Pitlochry–
Kirkmichael–Blairgowrie road. Pitlochry was on the Highland
Line while Blairgowrie had railway connection from 1855 to
1955. If you could get to Straloch from either station, perhaps by bicycle or hitch-hiking, Bynack could be reached via
Glen Fearnach rather than Glen Tilt. There was little to choose
between the two approaches in terms of distance, but the Fearnach approach had the advantage of going by Fealar Lodge at
the head of the glen.

On a broiling hot day early in June 1924, with extra-heavy packs,
a walk up Glen Fearnach from the Kirkmichael–Pitlochry road is
a sure test of fitness. But our hearts were light if our packs were
not, for had we not left behind degree examinations and all the
sedentary habits of college existence? Fealar provided us with a
glorious feast of sausages and, having sharpened our knives on
the huge grindstone, we struck across the hill and through the bog
to Bynack, where we stayed the night. Next day we reached our
destination – Corrour.

JH Malloy, Rucksack Club meet report, June 1924

After a week of walks in uninterrupted sunshine, including a trip
to Braemar to replenish supplies, Malloy's party of four continued
through the Lairig to catch the train home in Aviemore. Like Forest

Lodge in Glen Tilt, Fealar Lodge (NO 009800) remains in private hands and is still reached by private road up Gleann Fearnach.

> From Dundee the cheapest way to get to the Cairngorm Mountains is to push-cycle to Fealar via Kirkmichael and Glen Fearnach. Leaving Dundee on the 29th of June, the journey was easily accomplished and bread was got at Kirkmichael. Leaving the bicycles at Fealar, we reached Bynack that night and Corrour at midday on the 28th.
>
> A Neil Milne, Rucksack Club meet report, June 1925

June was as hot in 1925 as it had been in 1924 and, like their club companions of the previous year, Milne and his fellow cyclist spent several days at Corrour enjoying walks in glorious sunshine, including a return day-walk to Aviemore for provisions.

Yet another way of reaching Corrour was to begin by taking the train from Dundee to Kirriemuir, which had railway connection from 1861 to 1965.

> Left Dundee by the 9.13am train to Kirriemuir and set out to walk up Glen Clova to Braedownie [at the road-end]. A friendly van relieved us of our packs just outside Kirriemuir. We reached Braedownie about 4pm. After a long rest and a hearty meal we then set out up Glen Doll and over Jock's Road. We attempted to climb Lochnagar that night but owing to darkness gave up. We reached Callater at 3.00am and camped for the rest of the night.
>
> [The following day] We reached Braemar at noon, where stores were taken in, and after a lovely walk reached Derry Lodge at 6pm. Here we had tea and then set out for Corrour, which we reached about 9pm.
>
> AG Hill, Rucksack Club meet report, July 1930

On the following day, the party climbed over Ben Macdui to the Shelter Stone and returned to Corrour via the Lairig, and on the day after that they 'bade a fond farewell to Corrour' and left for home.

With improving roads and a greater number of vehicles on them, which if nothing else made hitch-hiking easier, Linn of Dee near Braemar gradually became the standard starting point for the walk-in to Corrour. For a while cars could be driven further, to Derry Lodge, but the vehicle track was closed to the public in 1931 owing to interference with estate activities. In 1938, 19-year-old Syd Scroggie and his 16-year-old companion used this approach even though lack of funds meant cycling the whole way from Dundee.

> We had cycled up from Dundee in a thunderstorm, St Elmo's Fire flickering blue on our handlebars, shared with midges a soaking camping place at Inverey, dumped our bikes at Derry Lodge, and trudged to a bog-girt Dee which in those days had to be forded or not crossed at all.
>
> Syd Scroggie, *The Cairngorms Scene and Unseen*, 1989

Syd's reminiscence highlights one major problem for all the early approaches to Corrour. Even the standard approaches along the Lairig Ghru from north or south required major river crossings.

BUILDING BRIDGES

ON THE NORTHERN approach from Aviemore the main obstacle was Am Beanaidh, named Allt na Beinne Moire on older maps. This drains the enormous trench of Gleann Eanaich and is the river into which the Allt Druidh flows on the north side of the Lairig. During Corrour's early days it was spanned by a succession of wooden bridges, each of which tended to be washed away by floods.

In 1912, the Cairngorm Club built the steel bridge that still stands (NH 926078). Modern OS maps name it the Cairngorm Club Footbridge, although originally it was more commonly known as the Iron Bridge. At the time, it was a major undertaking for the club, costing £94 4s 6d to build. In 2012, to celebrate its centenary, it was repainted and its plaques refurbished.

The only other problematic river crossing on the Aviemore approach was the Dee crossing opposite Corrour itself (see next section).

The southern approach from Linn of Dee has historically been more hazardous because it required no less than five major river crossings:

(1)   River Dee at Linn of Dee (NO 062896)
(2)   Lui Water in Glen Lui (NO 063914)
(3)   Derry Burn at Derry Lodge (NO 040935)
(4)   Luibeg Burn (NO 013942)
(5)   River Dee opposite Corrour (NN 983956)

(1) There had been a wooden bridge at the Linn since the early 19th century. The first was destroyed by the great flood of 1829, known as the Muckle Flood, during which it was recorded that at Braemar, the Dee rose 15–16ft to a width of 130ft. The replacement

bridge was itself replaced by the current stone bridge in 1857, so the crossing was never a problem for anyone trying to reach Corrour after its construction in 1877.

(2) In Glen Lui, on the way from Linn of Dee to Derry Lodge, the route crosses the Lui Water. There was a footbridge here before the bothy was built, and this was at some point replaced by the vehicle bridge that still stands today, known as the Black Bridge (although no longer black). Again, this was already in place by the time Corrour was built.

(3) At Derry Lodge, originally built in the late 1700s, the Derry Burn and the Luibeg Burn join to form the Lui Water. There was originally a footbridge over the Derry Burn west of the lodge, above the confluence, giving access to the continuing Lairig Ghru route westwards on the north bank of the Luibeg Burn. A bridge over the Luibeg Burn a short distance along gave access to Luibeg Cottage (the keeper's house) on the south bank. Here also, in time, stood Bob Scott's Bothy, named after a 20th-century keeper well-known to mountaineers of the day. This bridge has long since disintegrated, as has another bridge over the Lui Water just south of the confluence, which gave alternative access to the bothy.

Luibeg Cottage now has no bridge access and, like Derry Lodge, is currently unoccupied and maintained watertight by the estate. Following fires, Bob Scott's Bothy was rebuilt on the east side of the Lui Water, about 300m south of Derry Lodge, and now requires no bridge for access (NO 042932).

Current access to the Lairig Ghru path on the north side of the Luibeg Burn is by a footbridge over the Derry Burn just beyond (north of) Derry Lodge. A former bridge here was destroyed by floods in August 2014 but replaced in April 2015 by the Scottish Rights of Way Society as a memorial to one-time society president Donald Bennet.

In 2016, the NTS submitted plans to transform Derry Lodge into a basic mountain hostel, with additional public toilet facilities at the green barn beside it. Further plans involve rerouting the path to the Lairig Ghru. Currently, as the path to the Lairig heads west from the lodge along the north bank of the Luibeg Burn, it crosses a boggy area known as Derry Flats – an important lek (courtship and mating ground) for Black Grouse. It is proposed to build a bridge over the Lui Water south of the lodge, run a new path past the old Luibeg Cottage site and bridge the Luibeg Burn to regain the north side beyond the Flats.

(4) Bridging the Luibeg Burn further west, as it flows down from Coire Sputan Dearg of Ben Macdui, has proven even more problematic over the years as wooden footbridges here have always been in danger of being destroyed by floods. In CCJ No 16 (1901) Alexander Copeland described the then wooden plank bridge as 'picturesque'. Two years later, in SMCJ Vol 7 (1903), it was described as 'dilapidated'.

In 1948, two years before he led the renovation of Corrour Bothy, George Taylor built a more substantial bridge here. In the post-war years, steel could only be purchased with a licence, so the Luibeg Burn bridge became one of the first in Britain to be built of aluminium. This had the added advantage that, being lighter than steel, materials could be more easily taken to the site on the two-wheeled 'cartie' (push-cart) used for transportation. The bridge was named the Parker Memorial Bridge after engineer and Cairngorm Club member James Parker, who led the Ben Macdui indicator project in 1925 (see Page 50) and was Vice President from 1927–30.

One of Taylor's collaborators was Bill Ewen, who was Vice President of the Cairngorm Club at the time and a one-time walking companion of James Parker. On one occasion, Bill was walking with him with his hands in his pockets 'when suddenly Parker boomed "Take your hands out of your pockets, Ewen. Dashed levity! Showing off!"' (as told by Bill's son Innes).

On August 13–14 1956, the bridge was washed away by a cloudburst and carried 100m downstream, but in 1957 it was rescued, straightened, repaired and re-erected over a rocky gorge above the floodline 200m upstream, where it still stands. At the bridge's original location, the river can be crossed on stepping stones at low water, but the new location offers a permanent fail-safe dryshod crossing.

As a schoolboy in 1957, Innes Ewen helped Taylor carry materials to the new bridge site.

> On one occasion I was walking up the path alongside George when he confided in me that as well as the usual half-bag of cement, unbeknownst to the owner he had slipped a very large heavy steel wrench into their rucksack. On opening my rucksack at the bridge site I discovered that I was the lucky person.
>
> Innes Ewen, 'Before the Mountain Bothies Association',
> MBA Journal, Spring 2019

Before the Derry Burn and Luibeg Burn bridges were built, bothiers heading to Corrour could avoid them by taking the White Bridge route. This bridge was in existence to serve Bynack Lodge and even more remote Geldie Lodge, now both in ruin, before Corrour was built. Early bothiers arriving from Blair Atholl via Glen Tilt or Glen Fealar therefore didn't have to ford the Dee here, while the alternative route from Linn of Dee doesn't need to cross the bridge as it keeps to the near side of the river.

For further information and pictures of the history of Derry Lodge and the Luibeg Burn bridge, see Innes Ewen's YouTube site: www.youtube.com/watch?v=2YLgdm8uF2w.

Once into the heart of the Lairig Ghru, whether approaching Corrour from north or south by whatever route, there remains one final major crossing of the Dee.

THE DEE CROSSING

THE DEE TUMBLES down from its source at the Wells of Dee on the Braeriach plateau and gathers water fast as it flows through the gaping trough of Garbh Coire. In spate, by the time it reaches Corrour, it can be waist-high. Yet it has to be crossed to reach the bothy, which is situated on the opposite bank of the river to the Lairig Ghru path, 250m from the riverbank.

Before there was a bridge the ford was notorious. Not only was the bothy difficult or sometimes impossible to reach, but simply locating the building in darkness or inclement weather could be problematical, as VA Firsoff discovered in the 1930s.

> There was some exchange of opinions about the exact location of Corrour Bothy, which was very difficult to spot – a large grey boulder among many smaller grey boulders.
>
> VA Firsoff, *On Foot in the Cairngorms*, 1965

If the bothy was inhabited, kindly folk would place a candle in the window for the benefit of late arrivals.

> Arrived in darkness from Braemar and almost lost the bothy, although we both knew Corrour well. In thankfulness, placed candle in window for other travellers.
>
> CW Murray, 29 December 1953

In the SMC journal of 1913, with a degree of schadenfreude, James Parker recounted a crossing of the river after the first ascent of the Black Pinnacle in Braeriach's Coire Bhrochain.

> On reaching the river, two of the party walked through it at once; but the other two, disliking its appearance and apparently forgetting the fact that rivers increase in volume the further they are followed from their source, kept on the right bank, vainly endeavouring to

find an easy crossing. The reason they gave was that walking on the right bank was much better than that on the left bank. They did not explain how they were in a position to say so, but it was evident that the alleged superiority of their path vanished at the instant it dawned on them that the river was really getting too formidable. Unfortunately for the spectators on the left bank, they crossed without untoward incident.

James A. Parker, 'The Black Pinnacle of
Coire Bhrochain, Braeriach',
SMCJ Vol XII, 1913

In June 1924, two Rucksack Club members made the most of a week without rain at Corrour to improve the crossing.

A sun dial was drawn out in front of the bothy and a ford of stepping stones was made across the Dee just opposite, the latter a piece of work entailing a fair amount of labour while standing up to the knees in icy cold water.

Neil Milne and Ernest Jaff, Rucksack Club meets book,
June 1924

A few years later, their efforts were rewarded with a mention in the first Scottish Mountaineering Club Guidebook to the Cairngorms.

If the Dee is low, stepping stones may be found; otherwise the stream must be waded.

Henry Alexander, *The Cairngorms*, 1928

Even if you made it across the river, you still had 250m to go to the bothy.

We gain the western bank and pick our way as carefully as possible through the peat bog lying between it and the Corrour Bothy, and affording an unlimited amount of fuel to the Hospice. There are several big and deep pools in this mossy bog, none of which we would care to fathom by our legs in the dark.

Alexander Copeland, 'Cairn Toul and its Corries',
CCJ No 16, 1901

It is still the case today that, if you miss the path in darkness or in snow, reaching the bothy can be a messy affair. No stepping stones could tame a raging Dee and the bothy's visitors' books are full of tales of adventurous crossings, some humorous, others less so.

Arrived here from Braemar at 10.30pm. The Dee is very high – stepping stones covered. One of the party fell in and drifted downstream on his back.

3 May 1929

Arrived here in pitch darkness after slipping off the ford into the Dee and losing myself among the bogs below the bothy.

A Tewnion, 12 August 1939

We had to strip for the crossing. However, the bathe was quite refreshing, if a little cold. When is a bridge going to be built across this part of the river? Whose is the responsibility? I'm claiming damage for the loss of ten toes and if the river had been any wider I should be claiming for the loss of two feet – nipped off by ice-cold water.

WS Forgan, 27 April 1940

In April 1949, Adam Watson arrived with an English honeymoon couple.

> At Corrour the Dee was high and we had to wade through cold water but it was refreshing once the circulation returned. Mr Turner crossed with his pack, back for his wife, and crossed with her on his back.
>
> Recalled by Adam Watson in *It's a Fine Day for the Hill*, 2011

That Cairn Toul's easy we won't deny,
We did it in hours one, two, three.
But the greatest trial's yet to come.
We've got to cross the Dee.

James DK Johnston, 13 May 1949

A winter crossing, when the Dee was frozen, was often easier.

> We proceeded over the peat bogs and hags surrounding the bothy, which all lay blanketed in deep soft snow, and reaching the frozen Dee walked northwards on this splendid highway. The channel is

on average 15 feet in width, and in some parts was not entirely frozen, and, standing on the ice bridges, we could see the dark boulder bottom of the stream through the crystal-clear though turbulent water.

'A Winter Climb on Ben Macdhui', *Dundee Courier*,
7 January 1926

Lovely weather, bright sunshine and blue sky; everything under snow except the bothy, even the river, which we crossed dryshod and without even seeing it.

25 January 1951

Outside of winter, in 1950–1 the Dee seemed to be in spate more often than usual.

Once over the summit (*of the Lairig Ghru*) the snow got worse. It was very soft and we had to crawl over it in places. The blizzard increased from the Pools of Dee and by the time we were opposite the bothy we were wet to the skin, as wet as to wade through the Dee, which was in spate.

William DD Wallace, 9 April 1950

Conditions are very bad outside. An attempt was made by another party to cross the Dee without success. The water is running waist-high at its shallowest.

C Petrie, 26 September 1950

We found no stepping stones so we forded the icy waters at the shallowest point – waist high. Circulation was soon revived in the bothy.

Keith Whitelock, 15 May 1951

In contemplating crossing the Dee in spate:

Keep away frae hotels, said the cheery wee bloke,
Fur they're only looking fur people to soak.
Hoo sad tae relate ma spirits are broke,
Fur the Dee's a hotel and that is nae joke.

R McFaul, 27 June 1951

The dangers of the Dee crossing became national news when, on the September holiday weekend of 1950, it was the scene of a fatal accident. A party of six from the west of Scotland tried to ford the river some distance above the bothy in a severe storm. According to the Dundee Courier, they tried to cross 'by means of a hand chain bridge' (presumably holding hands).

In the raging torrent some lost their footing and all six men were hurled into the river.

'Torrent Breaks Hill Hikers' Hand-Bridge',
Dundee Courier, 27 September 1950

Five struggled out but the sixth man's body was later found 2½ miles downriver. The remaining men searched in vain for him before setting off through the Lairig Ghru for Aviemore in a blizzard of sleet. Near the summit of the pass, an exhausted second man died from heart failure.

THE HIMALAYAN BRIDGE 1951

FOLLOWING THE DOUBLE tragedy of 1950, in the summer of 1951, the Cairngorm Club, which had just finished renovating the bothy, spent a week building a bridge. Jack Milne was in charge of the project.

> The bridge was built to the same design as those used for crossing ravines in the foothills of the Himalayas, where Mr Milne had seen them forty years ago during leaves from the King's Dragon Guards.
>
> OCF, CCJ No 88, 1952

Fixed to wooden posts at either side, the bridge consisted of two wires, one for the feet and one for the hands. In the visitors' book, Jack Milne recorded work and life at the bothy.

July 2. Jack Milne and John Gadd arrived here to begin construction of a wire rope monkey bridge over the Dee.

July 3. Picked most favourable site for the bridge, where the river is narrowest, and the banks are highest and the most firm.

July 4. Cemented in one post four feet into the ground and cemented in accompanying stay-anchor. Cut and spliced stay-wire and dug second post-hole on near side of river. Gadd walked up to Garbh Coire Dhaidh and Fuar Garbhcoire, prospecting for new climbs. Climbed up to Angel's Peak via Chokestone Gully (still with hard snow inside).

July 5. Cemented in second post and stay anchor helped by Blair and Ruddiman. Had a really excellent social evening with Stanley, Finnigan, Thompson, Blair and Ruddiman, with much hilarity. It poured with rain all night and we went to bed in the early hours of –

July 6. Fixed and strained the foot and hand wires and tightened up stay wires. We only hope the parts stand the strain. The wires can be easily tightened. Finnigan, Stanley and Gadd went over to Bhrotain's Dee-face cliffs in the evening to see what they had to offer. Disappointed, no route of any length, but found a sporting corner and chimney on the central buttress about mid-height. Hard V. Diff. These cliffs would be better in rubbers on a dry day. Blair and Ruddiman brought up ten bottles of beer from Braemar – more hilarity – bed at 2am.

July 7. I'm sorry for falling asleep on the camp stool when the party was at its best. Again I thank everyone who has assisted me in ANY way. SAFE CLIMBING

Helpers A. Blair and RA Ruddiman had an equally busy week.

July 3. Arrived from Derry Lodge about 3pm bearing two camp stools, one card table and odd bits of bridge. Climbed Devil's Point in the evening – straight up the scree.

July 4. Walked into Aviemore for bread and groceries, only to discover it was early closing day. The proprietor of the 'Pot Luck' came to our rescue with a very welcome loaf... We got back to the bothy about 11.45pm.

July 5. Spent the morning cleaning up the bothy. In the afternoon we helped Jack and John complete the bridge.

July 6. Once more we were out of bread and this time we left for Braemar. We were lucky to meet the grocer's van at Derry Lodge & we were able to leave our groceries in Bob Scott's. In Braemar we made our big buy – 10 pints of beer, which we had to lug all the way back to the bothy, but oh boy! Was it worth it. Bed 2am.

On the 7th they 'spent a fairly lazy day', although still managing to do a few repairs to the bridge and climb The Devil's Point in the evening. On the 8th they left to explore further afield.

Helpers Stanley, Finnigan and Thompson also had a good time.

July 5. Stanley, Finnigan and Thompson walked down to Derry Lodge, where we borrowed two bicycles from Bob Scott. Thompson

successfully hitched a lift on a timber truck into Braemar, where he
retrieved another rather ancient bicycle belonging to Bob Scott. The
two others arrived later and we collected supplies and had an excellent
tea. We cycled back to Derry and en route saw a large herd of deer.
Ruddiman and Blair had hot tea waiting for us. We had an excellent sing-
song, which was much enhanced by Finnigan's inexhaustible supply of
songs. We bedded in at 1.30.

July 6. Today was a lazy day but marked the completion of the
bridge. Ruddiman and Blair brought more excellent beer back from
Braemar, which again led to an excellent evening.

July 7. We didn't get up till 10am. A very pleasant few days with
excellent companions.

The finished bridge was perhaps best described by Syd Scroggie
as 'somewhat perilous for the aged and nervous but highly stimulating for the acrobatic'. Blinded during the Second World War, he
returned to Corrour with companion Les Bowman in 1955.

> I had a bit of rope tied round my waist, and when I had got on to
> the bottom wire I clipped this bit of rope with me inside it to the
> top wire by means of the karabiner, leant back nonchalantly over
> the swirling water, supported by this sliding belay, and stretched
> my arms out wide. 'Les,' I yelled against the noise of the spate.
> 'Look, no hands.'
>
> Syd Scroggie, 'The Cairngorms: Scene and Unseen', 1989

Syd's happy experience of the bridge was almost a lone positive
one. As George Taylor pointed out in the 1961 Cairngorm Club
Journal, the bridge was never intended to be for anything other
than emergency use, but this not always appreciated in the days
and years that followed.

Several parties arrived and departed in flurries of spray, stray anoraks
and several near duckings from the Tibetan bridge.

12 July 1951

We were amongst the first to use the new rope bridge. I had left my
pack at the Tailors' Stone and Gil tried to cross with his pack as it
had all the grub in it. He got about two feet from the post when he

decided it wasn't safe so he got off and floundered through the Dee (boots an' a').

Jack H. Drummond and Gilmour Allan, 15 July 1951

It has been a lovely morning but I am not too pleased with our excursion so far as I fell in the stream about 5 miles back and consequently my kilt does not hang as well as it should… We had some small difficulty crossing the wire bridge as the 'foot' wire shot away from Jessie's feet and he was left kicking furiously. After tying himself in knots, falling over backwards and doing hand flips he managed, eventually and eventfully, to reach the other side.

18 July 1951

Arrived for a 'flying visit'. It seemed like that crossing the wire bridge!

Bob Alexander, 11 September 1951

War Office order 204/L/G re passage of troops over bridge (wire). Grab the top wire with the hands. At the same time lean chest on top wire. Feet together (boots highly polished) and leaning forward all the time. Proceed as rapidly as possible to the other side. If you lean backwards, compensation may be claimed from the nearest National Health Insurance Office.

Anonymous, 16 September 1951

Wire bridge no good for aged 9. I like my first visit to the Lairig.

Judith Findlay, 3 June 1953

Slept here and am going to climb Braeriach, returning here by Cairn Toul and Devil's Point. The wire bridge seems to have a grudge against me.

Shona Ackman, 2 September 1953

Disembowelled by hook on wire bridge.

Gillian Stephenson, 13 September 1953

What a bridge – all was going smoothly when the rucksack fell in.

Elizabeth Duncan, 17 September 1953

Crawled over in blazing heat from Derry to inspect wire bridge that Jack Milne and I put up three years back and surprised to find it in moderately good condition. Both wires very slack, however, and need readjustment. Have no tools with which to do the job, however, and as now domiciled in Nottingham they will have to remain slack (other CC members please note). As the bridge was for emergency use in floods, this matters little. Anyway, boulder hopping is less dangerous and more fun! Proceeding to Glen Geusachan to look for unscratched rock.

John Gadd (with Mrs JN Gadd), 26 July 1955

Arrived in blinding rain. Left five minutes later, still in blinding rain. Oh for the sunny south! Happy thought: as I can't get any wetter I'll be able to ford the Dee rather than bisect myself on the wire bridge. View from Devil's Point was stormy and magnificent.

R Kay, 26 August 1957

Defied death by crossing wire bridge with heavy rucksack.

25 October 1957

Arrived 5pm from Aviemore. Weather patchy. One of our members fell into the burn when that damn wire bridge broke. Rest waded across. We dragged the broken post up to the bothy to augment our firewood. O Thank God we took the trouble to bring logs. A howling wind and driving rain made sleep fitful. The door, though bolted, kept flying open. Climbed Devil's Point in the afternoon when the mist had cleared, only to be caught in a blizzard. Our stay was quite enjoyable.

Iain Morton, 26 March 1959

THE STEEL BRIDGE 1959

WITH THE WIRE bridge broken, the Nature Conservancy, a government body that had designated Mar Lodge Estate as a national nature reserve, decided to build not just a new, more permanent structure at Corrour, but five other bridges elsewhere on the estate. They turned to George Taylor, who had built the 1956 Luibeg Burn bridge, for advice. He agreed to design and build the bridges only after he'd learned he could have use of a helicopter to transport materials. In the event he built steel bridges at Corrour and Derry Dam and an aluminium bridge over the Glas Allt. Of the three other bridges to be built of wood, the estate objected to two and only the Etchachan bridge was built (to ease access to the Hutchison Memorial Hut in Coire Etchachan, which Taylor had built in 1957).

Taylor described the unique design he chose for Corrour as a 'tied arch'. If a single steel rib had been used to span the 48ft gap over the river between east and west abutments, it would have been awkward and heavy, making it difficult both to transport by helicopter and to manhandle. Instead two smaller ribs were joined in an inverted V-shape over the centre of the river.

Work began in heavy rain in July with the drilling of holes in the rock for the bridge foundations. Taylor's tent was ripped to pieces in a gale, but the weather improved after that. With the help of a handful of workers, a makeshift scaffolding was built in the middle of the river to facilitate the construction of the central join. All the work was completed in 15 days. Returning visitors were quick to express their thanks for the new bridge.

At least we don't run the risk of drowning, now that there's a bridge. My sincerest thanks.

Sirdar Denoon, 10 July 1959

Congratulations on a fine bridge.

Pat Butcher, 7 August 1959

For first-time visitors, the bridge was immediately taken for granted, as it is today. The difficulty of the Dee crossing became of historical interest only and, after decades of mishap and tragedy, the whole matter was soon considered no longer worthy of further mention in the visitors' books... except by those who couldn't find the bridge.

Missed footbridge and spent half an hour looking for it in almost total darkness. Arrived Corrour via 20 bogs at 11.30pm.

David Simpson, 13 May 1966

In the 2000s, the boggy path from the Lairig Ghru path to the bridge and bothy was improved and the junction is now cairned and so obvious that, hopefully, no one can miss it.

But if the Dee doesn't get you...

[An Edinburgh man] 35, slipped and fell while crossing small stream behind Corrour Bothy. Received slight head and back injuries. Evacuated by helicopter.

25 June 1978 (reported in CCJ No 98, 1978)

CORROUR THROUGH EXPERIENCE

HAPPY TO BE HERE

A PRIMITIVE REFUGE such as Corrour would not be most travellers' first choice of overnight accommodation, but it has one unique selling point – its location at the heart of prime real estate. As further attraction, guests stay for free. Throw in the odd Cairngorm storm raging outside and its lack of amenities can seem relatively unimportant.

Thoughtfully situated in the country, a day from every human habitation, no golf course but every modern convenience.

4 May 1928

We went to seek the Angel's Peak
But a gale is blowing there.
Yet we have food and life is good
So what are we to care.

Alexander PM Donald, 6 August 1928

They talk about a 'Home from Home'
While this is not exactly THAT.
There's certain comfort here for those that roam.
There's shelter when you're weary, wittles when you're short,
A bed which might be better, fuel of a sort.
There's whiles a muse, they say, and though there's not a cat,
I haven't seen or heard a single – or a married – rat.
For which we'll thank the Lord, so THAT IS THAT.

25 August 1928

Wittles is a Dickensian word for vittles, ie food.

It's the best Sunday I've spent as yet amongst the hills. I think it's grand.

8 August 1929

Stay, weary climber, and rest thy bones
Either on the heather or cold flagstones.
The fire is burning clear and bright.
Surely to Christ! You'll stay the night?

12 July 1931

I've been in Skye, I've been in Ross,
And suffered many a chilly doss.
But upon this you can be sure,
There's none to beat dear old Corrour

'Ptarmigan', 16 July 1931

The small library of Corrour Bothy is most interesting, especially
tonight to me, a lone wayfarer. The visitors' book is the best. Thanks
(very much) to the two scouts who have left. There was dry wood
and dry heather a-plenty to keep going a roasting fire… Corrour
Bothy, only one of its kind in the world, is as comfortable – and nae
sae pernickety – as, say, the Savoy Hotel.

J Chisholm Mair, 13 August 1931

Ne'er did Corrour look half so sweet
As when viewed from Macdui with freezing feet.
Darkness descending,
Mist impending,
Hasten me down with foot so fleet
Into the bothy's safe retreat.

E Rothney, 3 October 1931

A perfect day – a perfect night.

S Arnott, 1 August 1937

Unbroken blue sky, merciless sun, wonderful moonlit night.
Tomorrow I must needs me hie back to Braemar and
civilisation – regretfully.

Dark night weighs down the forest bough,
Strange shapes go flitting through the gloom,
But see – a spark, a flame.
And now the wilderness is home!

JA Horne, 12 April 1938

This is my first visit to the Cairngorms and the only way I can express myself is to say I'm glad I'm Scotch.

Bill Simpson, 14 August 1942

The solitude of this lonely bothy never fails to inspire me with a hope and a joy which is non-existent in the towns.

The way was long, the sun was hot,
A gurgling stream our only thought,
The hills above us towering high,
Reaching out to a deep blue sky.
Then, at the foot of the 'Devil's' tower,
The oasis for climbers, the lonely Corrour.
Dwarfed by the hills, it was standing there,
Barren and desolate, lonely and bare,
But who could despise it, yes who could despise
This refuge from snow and the rain and the flies.

Ronnie MacDonald, 16 July 1949

The longer I stayed, the better I liked it!

Gary Steiger, 11 July 1951

When roads are rough and weather cold
The misty clouds begin to lour
The rain can daunt a walker bold
And Paradise is called Corrour

A Millet, 27 July 1953

In wind, rain, snow and slush,
Better two in a bothy than two in a bush.

R. Rochester, who lived here during two days of such weather, 15 August 1956

Having spent two nights here, one with Mr Woolridge as a companion and the second with the ever-hopeful mouse, Tony and I both feel we couldn't have chosen a better place than Scotland in which to spend our honeymoon. And so we continue towards the sunset of the American travelogue (really the misty tops of the Braeriach and Cairn Gorm mountains).

Jay and Tony Lyon, 12 August 1957

From out of the misty hills we tramped,
Hungry, cold and very damp,
When there across the Dee we did espy
The Corrour Bothy, firm and dry.
From there the Cairngorms we did see.
An ideally placed bothy I think you'll agree.

P Atkinson, 28 August 1957

Arrived from Aviemore at 6pm after camping twice in the Lairig Ghru
and climbing Cairn Toul. The greatest scenery I have ever seen. Good
luck to anyone who stops at this spot in paradise.

R Browning, 4 July 1958

Arrived for one night in this palatial residence via Loch Einich,
Braeriach and Cairn Toul (bathed in genuine 100% liquid sunshine all
the way). Back to the jungles of civilisation tomorrow. Thank God for
Corrour. As long as it's here I can always look forward to a couple of
days in the company of great friends.

AG Haddon, 23 August 1958

Tramping the range of the Cairngorm,
I sought this bothy to keep warm,
And rested here one full clear day
Before wending on my errant way.
I was not asked for any money
(Being in Scotland you might think that funny!).
All that was expected of me
In return for hospitality,
To clean the mess after my suppers
And so help the other follow-uppers.

Fred Cowan, 3 October 1959

Thursday. Been wandering on the Cairngorms in the rain since
Monday. This magic wee bothy is a great relief from the weather and
midges. We saw a 'moonbow' at night up the Lairig Ghru and deer
came very close. A magical place.

Cy and Dan, 29 August 1996

Excellent day yesterday
Excellent day today
Excellent bothy
Excellent bottle of Pittvaich last night
Excellent life

Mark, 5 September 1996

Reached this bothy about 1600 hours after a grand walk through the
Lairig Ghru... The last walkers passed through about 1800 hours and
then I was all alone. After numerous cups of soup and a meal I settled
down for the evening. Sitting in my sleeping bag by the window,
reading a wonderful book called 'Notes from a Small Island' by Bill
Bryson. What better place to read it.

As light failed I lit the night lights and sat surrounded by a
warm flickering glow, the rain lashing the roof and the wind tearing
down the valley. Six deer walked past and two mice came in to
say hello.

...

The rain is coming in waves down the valley, the wind is trying hard
to take the roof off the bothy, water is cascading in long white streaks
off the slopes of Carn a' Mhaim and there is fresh snow on Cairn
Toul. Who said July was a <u>summer</u> month? As I sit here I can hear the
water dripping down the chimney and if I close my eyes it sounds like
logs spitting on an open fire.

I don't think I want to be anywhere else just now. The company of
a friend would make it a touch better and perhaps stop me rambling
on in this book. The weather can do what it likes here, I am happy
and content.

Antony Wiles, 1 July 1997

From Rothiemurchus Lodge we came
Through Braeriach, Cairn Toul and hills with no name.
With early hilltops hidden in a shroud
We stepped out first in scudding cloud.
The day grew brighter as we came on through,
With Scotland's beauty revealed to view.

After a mountain day that will be hard to beat
We arrived at the bothy with weary feet,
A welcome sight down here below.
Thanks to those who keep it so.

Dave and Jane Green, Northern Ireland, 21 May 1998

Squelch, squelch, slip, splash, b------s, squelch, slip, splash, splash,
b------s, squelch.
'You know, I can see a wee lump in the middle of my field of vision.'
'Mmm?'
   'Now, I canna tell in the pitch blackness. It could be a tuft of heather,
   it could be a rock, it could be a mountain or it could be a bothy.'
'Mmm?'
'It's a bothy!'
'A BOTHY! A BOTHY!'
'We made the bothy!'
'BOTHY, BOTHY, BOTHY!'
'HOORAY!'

15 November 1998

Walked in with son Will to spend first ever night in a bothy. Stunning
views on the walk in and the sight of a few deer made it even better.
Just great to walk using a map with no roads showing – no phone
signal (good) and all the basics here. Just a great experience that now
I am over 60 has to go down as something to do with a bucket list.

Alan, 22 January 2016

What a treat! Corrour Bothy is amazing. I was alone for two nights,
but it was still a pleasure. What an amazing place, and what an
awesome job the MBA do. THANK YOU!

Ben, 25 February 2016

Had an amazing chat with 3 experienced hikers by firelight in an
amazing valley. Undoubtedly one of the best experiences of my life.

Luke, Tom, Gregory, Joe, all 16 years old, first hike, 8 July 2016

This bothy saved my life in so many ways. Not only was I almost dying
of hypothermia. I finally got to kiss the man I love. The fire and his
warmth kept me going. I will be forever grateful.

M Snaith, 17 July 2016

MIXED BLESSINGS

NOT EVERYONE WHO stays at Corrour is entirely won over by its charms.

Back to that elusive, excellent and elevating odour, that sweet blending of venerable cheese, fragrant heather and ancient pine.

25 June 1929

Here's to you and here's to me
And here's to them who like it
But as sure as I see the silvery Dee
To get here you have to hike it.

8 September 1929

I am feeling much better for my trek among the wonderful hills, but owing to sleeping and walking in damp clothes for 4 days I have contracted a cold in the stomach and feel pain all over when I eat (this, however, does not prevent me from eating!!).

12 June 1931

Another rotten day! Pouring as usual, accompanied by a howling wind. Supplies running out. The Dee's well up today after all the rain and it is going to be difficult to cross without swimming... We are all feeling pretty miserable about having to return to civilisation after such a pleasant few days in the Gorms.

John HL Innes, 21 August 1931

There is sure no place like this – this side of hell.

19 September 1931

Beastly weather, low mist, strong wind and rain. Have had a very enjoyable walk.

GL Middleton, 14 June 1936

Bothy as draughty as ever... Was thoroughly soaked on arrival and
lashing rain did not permit an excursion for wood... Turned into my
sleeping bag as the only warm spot... Have learned that winter kit
should be carried all the year round in the Gorms as I have been much
warmer here in mid-winter. I am leaving in the bothy trousers as my
own are still wet. Fair exchange is no robbery.

David Browning, 29 May 1938

The 'bothy trousers'?!

Back again. Good Heavens. Swore I would never come here again.
Wet clothes. Sore feet. What a life!

5 May 1940

Our feet are wet, we haven't any sandwiches and we want to
go home.

Mary S. Bassett with Cathie Meldrum, 7 July 1940

Two weary hikers had meant to go from Aviemore to Derry Lodge,
but passing here at 6.00pm were unable to resist temptation and
stayed here for the night. Heather and an old log saved us from death
by freezing (only just).
'Blessed is he that expecteth little,
For he shall not be disappointed.'

JWE Nisbet, 23 September 1942

I came, I don't come back. (J. Scobbie)
15 miles which felt like 115. (JA Dick)
I go, I no come back. (R. Greig)

27 July 1949

Arrived up here just over a week ago and have been staggering
round these hills ever since – cursing the boulders and the weather
(mist & rain). Here at long last I've seen why the hills fascinate some
people. The view down the lairig tonight is superb – lovely purple
hills topped with large white clouds set in a deep-blue sky – one of
the finest sights I've seen.

Richard Past, 21 August 1950

Apart from:

Things that go 'bang' in the night,
Doors that open of their own accord,
Men that snore,
Women that talk in their sleep,
Mice that hold track races round sleeping bags,
Inadequate library for bedtime reading,
u. s. w.

We bestow our fondest love on the builders of this place.

Loraine, 22 August 1957

'usw' = 'und so weiter' (German for 'and so on').

Arrived from Aviemore to sleep in cotton sleeping bags – mad
fools! Plans for assault on peaks frustrated by low drizzling mist –
most unpleasant morning. Cairngorm! O Cairngorm! How you have
fulfilled all our expectations. We were told you were indifferent
to those who chose to invade your sacred precincts, but this is
carrying it too far. We haven't seen a single peak – alas, alack! Two
innocent (!) Welshmen representing their nation in their fellow
Celtic land of Scotland, and the fates bring mist.

Bryan Roberts and Arnold Jones, 10 August 1958

Arrived here last night – pitch black and pouring rain – never been so
thankful to see this place – many thanks.

I stood in the Lairig at midnight,
When a thought came into my head,
What a fool I was to be standing there,
When I might have been in bed.

BH Harrison, 3 October 1958

Called in at 4pm with a boot full of blood from camp at Luibeg.
Memoir to other 'happy campers' – if you want to dance around in
bare feet, don't jump on empty fruit salad tins.

Bloody boot wearer J. Kincaid, Elastoplasts stuck on by
AJ Colman, 29 August 1959

Spent 4 nights here. Caught a cold. Why I did not stay at home I do
not know.

M Holliday, 24 September 1959

Arrived here last night at 10.00pm, footsore and weary, suffering
under a 40lbs load (400 days food and 18 sweaters – I thought it
would be cold and snowy). Thank goodness for the lights in the bothy
or I would never have found the place – and oh! My feet!! Blisters
weighing pounds each.

3 October 1959

Had a spiffing day with my good friends. Weather has been spiffing.
Everything has been spiffing. The colour of heather is a pleasure
to the eye – what a sight. Saw a lovely bunny today, skipping along.
It really was lovely.

6 July 1980

This prompted the following reply.

Had a b----y terrible day today. Climbing hills all b----y day. B----y
waste of time. B----y got soaked.

6 July 1980

As we left Shiel Bridge at the start of this foolishness, an upmarket
chap said to us 'Tell me, why do you do this?' At the time we had no
suitable answer. And now here at Corrour, after wind (thanks to Raven
Foods Ltd), condensation, sole-destroyed feet and a body that feels as
though it's been on the rack, I must admit I haven't a f-----g clue!

15 May 1981

Sob. Sob. My life now lies in the flickering broken flame of the bothy
candle (all two inches of it).

26 May 1982

If I were not paid to relate the truth in these surveys, by my deepest
convictions I would publicly, widely, loudly advocate that this ludicrous
landscape be de-bouldered, ploughed, sown and mown into bowling-
green grassland free to the access of push-chairs, shopping trollies and
normal folk with normal joints. Who are the maniacs and where are the
damned liars who describe this God- and man-forsaken place as 'Heaven'?

To stumble and squelch along abused and treacherous paths; to spend evenings hunched over a sputtering and inadequate stove before an old and derelict fireplace; is that heaven? Where is the joy in fending off eternal swarms of carnivorous insects so dense that they shame the plagues of Moses?

Fie on you grinning idiots who take pleasure in this special hell. And the rain! The ceaseless rain! Oh God!

Theo (1st night of 4, under sufferance),
20 August 1996

The midges are biting. Up to me knees in mud. Wonderful!

Eddie and Anne, 22 August 1998

Some women get whisked off to the Maldives for their honeymoon. I get to sleep in a mountain bothy! Great stay, everything's clean and tidy, love the toilet! Thank you for maintaining!

Francesca, 24 July 2016

THE WAR YEARS 1939–45

THE SECOND WORLD WAR inevitably saw less footfall at Corrour. The records of clubs such as the Rucksack Club illustrate some reasons why, with reduced club membership and increased travel difficulties.

> Mr Rennie Stewart pointed out that owing to the rationing of petrol the club was going to have difficulty in holding the usual meets. He suggested that if the club membership could be raised to twenty, a bus might be hired for a day. He asked the members present to do all they could towards increasing the number in the club.
>
> Minutes of Rucksack Club meeting, 9 November 1939

In the event the club managed only two meets that academic year.

> Unfortunately the war has restricted our activities, weekend meets being impossible due to lack of petrol. Inquiries about private buses were made, but the costs were exorbitant. Nevertheless, two very successful meets were held, the first in December at Clova YH, the second at Easter in Crianlarich YH.
>
> Rucksack Club Secretary's Report on Session 1939–40

Matters deteriorated even further as the war progressed.

> The AGM of the club was held on Saturday. About a dozen members attended. There were no women present.
>
> Minutes of Rucksack Club AGM, 11 November 1943

In the months leading up to the war, German imperialism was never far from the minds of some visitors to Corrour.

Struggling along the Lairig Ghru through 4 hours' steady rain, on my first hike for 8 years, I finally began to tell myself that there was no

Corrour, never had been one, that it was only a myth invented to
delude innocents like me. Well, there is a bothy, although it hasn't much
lebensraum, there was no irredentism in it and we were made quite
welcome… Vive la bothy! Estas bona loko!

George Gilfillan, 16 July 1939

The need for 'lebensraum' (living space) was the pretext used by
Hitler to expand the German state by invading neighbouring territories. 'Irredentism' is the policy of claiming or reclaiming territory
that was once part of the state or is seen to be because of common
(eg linguistic) ties.

Just before the outbreak of war an intriguing signature was left
in the visitors' book by one of the bothy's first European visitors.

[No entry]

Aleksander Aleksandrowisz, Wilno, Poland, 24 July 1939

With no message left for us, one wonders what his story was.
Germany invaded Poland on 1 September 1939 and exiled Polish
air squadrons later received training in the Highlands.

Once the war began, there were new concerns for those who
made it to Corrour.

The time is just after midnight and not being able to get any sleep
because I can't buck the heat, I'm sitting literally 'up the lum' and
with as cheery a fire as I can manoeuvre and most unpatriotically
forgetting the 'blackout'.

Lilian M Cameron, 9 August 1940

Spent the night in the bothy and am now on my way to Braemar via
the Linn. Oh! By the way. A plane passed over the bothy last night –
the majority of the temporary inhabitants of the bothy believe it was
a 'Jerry' and a hastily improvised blackout was improvised.

Dan G Walker, 3 August 1940

The plane was almost certainly British. During the Second World
War, air crews were trained in the Cairngorms for continental raids.
On the summit plateau of Ben Macdui, 300m NW of the summit
cairn is a memorial to the five crew members of an Avro Anson that
crashed here during training in 1942. Other crash sites are dotted
around the Cairngorm plateaus.

Some who reached Corrour voiced their views on the futility of war, often couched in socialist terms fostered by the depression of the 1930s.

The early thirties brought hard times, unemployment or dead-end jobs. Just to have a job was happiness. Yet people had hopes for the future. They discussed utopias and political solutions. Fellow climbers went off to fight for the republicans in the Spanish Civil War... Climbing was a healthy outlet at that time. We climbed for adventure because we needed it.

Jock Nimlin, reported in *Weir's Way*, 1981

This being my first trip into 'The Gorms', it's quite a pity that all the others who have spent nights in the Lairig should be caught up in a war of greed and should give this all up for those who never appreciate us.

Roderick MacDonald, 10 June 1940

I arrived at the bothy to find it empty; there was a time you could depend on seeing someone here but I suppose that most of the people who visit here have been compelled to go to war and fight for somebody else's property. Some will come back here, others won't. I think it's time we put a stop to these wars, and until we get a new, better system these wars will always go on. I had a good walk from Glenmore Lodge over Cairn Gorm, down to the Shelter Stone, up the Feith Buidhe, on to Ben Macdhui, down the Allt Clach nan Taillear and into the old doss. Tired but happy. Peace to all workers. Unite.

Dick Gowers, Creag Dhu, 12 June 1940

On the other hand, many visitors wanted to forget the war by escaping to a bothy retreat that provided more than enough distractions. One such visitor was a young Tom Weir (1914–2006), who would go on to become one of Scotland's best-known mountaineers, writers and broadcasters and the first recipient of the John Muir Trust Lifetime Achievement Award.

The fateful calling-up papers had arrived and I calculated that, if the firm let me leave on Saturday, I should have just four days of freedom before being engulfed in the army... I would go to the hills and forget the war in the short glory of peace... Where should I go? Of all the Ordnance Survey maps I know there is none so compelling as the Cairngorms... Dark clouds were piling on the hills but my heart was lighter than the rucksack and I stepped it out, impatient to get into the wilderness and among the pines.

Tom Weir, *Highland Days*, 1948

Another soldier took advantage of a day's leave to escape to the hills above Corrour.

Happy the man who in these days of stress has access to the great mountains, for thither he can escape for the day, and from the high inviolate places bring back a strength and a peace he can never find within 'the walls of cities barricaded evermore".
(*a quote from Wordsworth's poem 'The Recluse'*)
   So taking the poet's advice on my 24 hours off, I set out the other day by the foaming Linn and made my way up the glen of Dee... The hills greeted me smilingly as I walked to meet them.

From Corrour he climbed Cairn Toul, crossed the plateau to Braeriach, descended to the Pools of Dee and returned to Linn of Dee via the Lairig Ghru.

In my 24 hours off I spent a hundred years in the enchanted land of the hills. I had been where the White Presences are and the wind blows cold and clean and I returned to a tumultuous world with a new joy and a new peace in my heart.

'Escape: A Day in Highest Aberdeenshire',
The Press and Journal, Aberdeen,
JS Wood, 26 July 1943

[After a night at the Shelter Stone] Loch Avon looked grand in the sun and compared favourably with scenes abroad which are now 'verboten'. [*After arriving at the bothy*] Found supplies of ham, soup, bread & honey and coffee. Have now made my bed and am ready to lie on it. A few days away from work and air raids is much appreciated in these fine surroundings.

D Buckle, I September 1940

On examining supplies, found that most had been sampled by
the bothy mouse – bread, chocolate, cheese, oatcakes, maps and
margarine all suffered.

Jack Scroggie, 7 April 1940

20-year-old Jack (Syd's twin brother) later became a reverend
who lived to the age of 93. He would return to Corrour after the
war and so would Syd, although he didn't know he would lose his
sight to a mine and never see Corrour again when he wrote this.

On our way to Dundee after stay of 3 nights. No matter what the
league of bothy renovators say, the roof leaks. Beware the spot in the far
corner. Summit of Ben Macdhui in mist. Took a compass course south. In
10 seconds were going true north. Grey Man not at home.

Sydney Scroggie, 19 July 1939

Others never came back.

Best of luck and a safe return from the war to all those mountaineers
who are forced to go and fight on either side.

4 January 1940

Hear! Hear!

[added in margin]

These comments exemplify the fraternity that often existed
between mountaineers on opposite sides of the conflict. Pioneering Scottish climber Bill Murray wrote his classic book on 1930s
winter mountaineering on toilet paper in a prisoner-of-war camp.
He was captured during the North African campaign by a German
tank commander

He was a mountaineer. We both relaxed. He stuffed his gun away.
After a few quick words – the Alps, Scotland, rock and ice – he
could not do enough for me... We shared a beer and toasted
'Mountains'.

WH Murray, The Scotsman, 2 June 1979

For those who stayed at home and were able to reach the Cairngorms, the early years of the war saw heavy falls of snow that
provided superb winter adventure, both on foot and on ski.

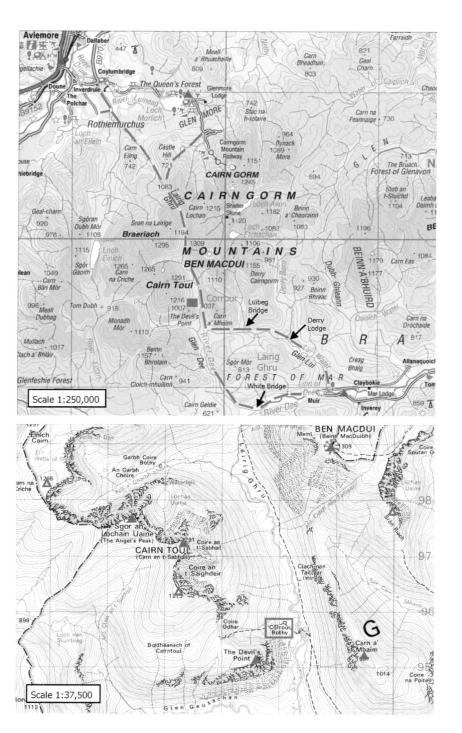

Scale 1:250,000

Scale 1:37,500

I

Looking across the Lairig Ghru to The Devil's Point (left) and Cairn Toul (right) from Carn a' Mhaim © Ralph Storer

Looking across the Lairig Ghru to Ben Macdui from The Devil's Point © Ralph Storer

Looking south over the summit of the Lairig Ghru to Cairn Toul from the Cairn Gorm–Ben Macdui Plateau © Ralph Storer

Looking south along the Lairig Ghru from the slopes of Braeriach, with Ben Macdui in the background © Ralph Storer

The Devil's Point towers over the River Dee above White Bridge © Ralph Storer

Looking north along the Lairig Ghru towards Cairn Toul and Braeriach © Ralph Storer

The Devil's Point towers over Corrour Bothy © Ralph Storer

Looking across the Lairig Ghru to Ben Macdui from Corrour Bothy, with the toilet extension in the foreground © Ralph Storer

Corrour Bothy interior: the sleeping platform © Ralph Storer

9

Corrour Bothy interior: the fireplace © Ralph Storer

Garbh Coire, with the semi-permanent snowbeds of Garbh Choire Mor centre left and Braeriach far right © Ralph Storer

10

11

Corrour Bothy in 1934 © Unknown

Corrour Bothy in 1950: pre-renovation inspection © Innes Ewen Archive

Corrour Bothy in 1950 after removal of the old roof © Innes Ewen Archive

Corrour Bothy in 1950: working on the new roof © Innes Ewen Archive

The Bren gun carrier on the moor in 1950 © Innes Ewen Archive

16

Corrour Bothy in 1950: after renovation. George Taylor is second from left © Innes Ewen Archive

17

Helicopter at the Dee bridge site in 1959 © Innes Ewen Archive

18

Carrying a rock drill to the Dee bridge site in 1959 © Innes Ewen Archive

19

Building the Dee bridge in 1959 © Innes Ewen Archive

20

The Dee bridge today © Ralph Storer

21

22

The bridge over the Luibeg Burn pre-1948 © Innes Ewen Archive

The cartie used to carry materials to the new Luibeg Burn bridge in 1948 © Innes Ewen Archive

Building the 1948 Luibeg Burn bridge © Innes Ewen Archive

23

24

The original 1948 Luibeg Burn Bridge site, with Ben Macdui behind © Innes Ewen Archive

25

The debris of the 1948 Luibeg Burn bridge after being washed a way in 1956 © Innes Ewen Archive

26

The Luibeg Burn bridge today on its 1957 site © Ralph Storer

28

The Derry Lodge bridge after being washed away in 2014 © Ralph Storer

29

The Derry Lodge bridge today, built in 2015 © Ralph Storer

Corrour Bothy on 3 April 1983, the morning after the tent-destroying storm © Ralph Storer

Reconstructing the toilet extension in 2018 © Neil Reid

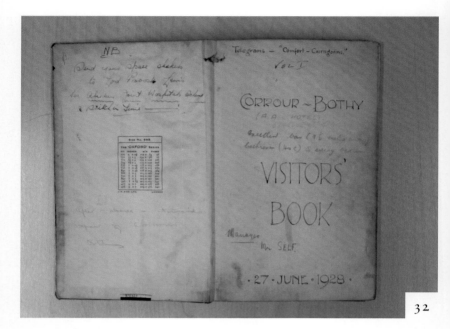

The first page of the first Corrour Bothy visitors' book, 27 June 1928 © from the vistors' books

July 6, 1930 © from the vistors' books

July 21, 1936 © from the
vistors' books

34

35

June, 1939 © from the vistors' books

15

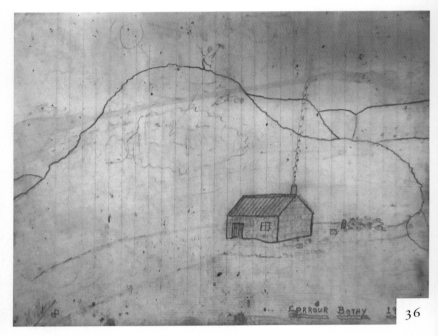

July, 1950 © from the vistors' books

1958 © from the vistors' books

On Sunday, April 12, 1942, Ben Macdhui was climbed in mist
(from Luibeg Bothy) via the Luibeg Burn... The run down was
slow at first, but improved as more crystalline snow was reached
on lower slopes. A hard overnight frost and a clear sky made the
running much faster on Monday. The rest of the week was perfect skiing weather, with frosty nights, a blazing sun by day and
practically no wind.

Tuesday night was spent at Corrour Bothy, and the following day
the cliff edge from Devil's Point to Cairn Toul and Angels Peak
was traversed, and finally a very fast run down from the latter to
the head of Glen Geusachan.

RO Scott, CCJ No 83, 1942–43

In the same month, another Cairngorm Club party was induced
by the fine weather to attempt Lochnagar on ski at night.

The full moon lit up the snow-covered mountain, which sparkled
myriad-pointed from myriads of snow crystals... There was no
whisper of wind; it was breathlessly beautiful... The summit of
Lochnagar was reached at dawn... It was exhilarating and the
beauty of it all defies description.

Mary Farquharson, CCJ No 83, 1942–43

One suspects the following visitor was less enamoured of his
stay at Corrour.

LOST: 1 pair field glasses in case, marked Nigeria Survey No 1. Please
return to –

AC Mackilroy, 29 June 1942

The most poignant visitors' book entries are from those who
looked forward to returning after the war but, for all we know,
may not have done.

Wilfred gave an amazing display of hand traverses on the wall below
the shelf (on The Devil's Point). He definitely has one route only,
as when I moved towards him he was forced to try a gully to the
west but had to descend again. He is indeed entertaining. Off now to
the Linn and so home now. Saturday to register – 'for my King and
Country need me'. So here's to the next time. Farewell, Corrour.

T Reid, 24 May 1940

This is my first,
But not my last.
In days to come
I hope to pass – this bothy.

George Avery, 4 June 1940

Arrived from Einich Lower Bothy via the tops. Spent the next day lounging about in the sun. Climbed Devil's Point in the evening to see the sunset. Leaving today for Beinn Ghlas in Glen Tilt. The weather has been too warm for climbing. Hope we outlast this war to visit the bothy again.

A Pringle, 16 June 1940

This visit carries out the promise to come again which I made when I came here June 1939, although when I wrote it then I never expected my next visit would be during a leave from the army. However, I'm still hoping to be back here for several days when the war is over.

C Drinkwater, 21 August 1940

Spent a very comfortable night here having been very much cheered on arrival to find the bothy in such a good condition, provisioned with victuals for the starving and dry heather for the weary.

It is a pity that other bothies have so suffered from the hands of those who have no appreciation of their worth and function, and their still-erect chimney-stacks stand as memorials to their vandalism and a reminder to all of us to conduct ourselves with sympathy, understanding and collaboration not only in the walks of the Cairngorms but in all the walks of life.

21 May 1943

And perhaps the most deceptively poignant of all the war years' entries...

TWO 'DANDY NINTHS' ARE WE
WHO WANDERED OFF THE BEAT
LYING ON THIS BOTHY FLOOR
AIN'T THIS LIFE A TREAT

TWO LONELY SOLDIERS A Matthew & D Winton,
7/9 R Scots, 24 June 1943

The 7th (Leith) and 9th (Highland) were battalions of the Royal Scots infantry regiment.

The loss of visitors' books for the years 1943–8 is unfortunate. In the later years of the Second World War, a company of the Canadian Forestry Corp set up a sawmill and lumber camp in Glen Lui to extract timber for the war effort, and some of the lumberjacks may well have made it to Corrour. The missing books would also cover the end of the war and the return of soldiers to the Cairngorms.

In a newspaper article near the end of the war, writer and mountaineer Janet Adam Smith explored her own feelings about returning to the hills of home.

> Being separated from mountains is like being separated from people. You think you are stoic and noble and disciplined; then suddenly you have the wildest longing to see a person come into the room, to hear a 'hullo' spoken by someone who is half a world away. It's like that with the unattainable mountains... I don't doubt that we shall find again in the hills the supremely happy moments we used to know, but they will not be the same moments as those we look back on; they will not exactly repeat the pre-war pattern. The companions, the surroundings, the places, one's own capacities – there will be change and loss in all these elements for most climbers.
>
> Janet Adam Smith, 'Return to the Hills',
> *The Listener*, 21 November 1944

More controversially, she went on to make a suggestion about Corrour Bothy that caused great debate at the time (and no doubt still would!).

> A hostel should be established on the site of Corrour Bothy, by the side of the Lairig Ghru, that grandest of all rights of way. I know that heroes have used the Corrour Bothy, as it stands, as a base. But I don't think that people are necessarily decadent if they prefer a slightly less rigorous lodging on their holidays than this doorless, floorless dwelling with the leaky roof... I know what the pessimists will say – a hostel in the heart of the Cairngorms would lead to swarms of trippers, ruin the peace of the hills, and demoralise climbers by making them too comfortable. I don't believe it: I have seen far too much of the unpretentious French

Alpine Club huts, which have produced none of these dire results. The frivolous Lowland trippers are not going to endure the three hours' heavy walking from the road-end in order to sleep in a bunk and eat the tinned soup and bully beef they have had to cart along with them. As for spoiling the peace and quiet, the Cairngorms are big enough and wild enough to make 30 extra climbers disappear from the landscape very easily. And as for spoiling the climber – nonsense. A hut built on the scale of one in the Alps of Savoy, with bunks, and opportunity for cooking your own food, and drying your clothes, would corrupt no climber. But it would open to him all sorts of new possibilities that, in present conditions, time usually forbids.

Janet Adam Smith, 'Return to the Hills',
The Listener, 21 November 1944

By the time the visitors' books pick up again in 1948, bothiers had put the war years behind them and moved on to the more mundane but, in peacetime, more important matters of shelter, warmth, comfort and mice.

As a coda to the Second World War years, in the 1960s, three overnight shelters were constructed by the military on the high plateau connecting Ben Macdui to Cairn Gorm and Beinn Mheadhoin. El Alamein (NJ 016053) and St Valery (NJ 001002), built to support cross-country skiing, honoured those who fought in those battles. Curran (NH 983010), built to aid mountain rescue, was named after the Royal Marine leader of the construction team.

In 1975, St Valery and Curran were demolished and El Alamein abandoned following the Feith Buidhe Disaster – Britain's worst mountaineering tragedy. In November 1971, five schoolboys and an assistant leader died in a blizzard when they attempted but failed to reach Curran. Only the leader and a sixth schoolboy survived the ordeal. To prevent a recurrence of the tragedy, it was decided that all high-level Cairngorm refuges should be removed.

BOTHY LIFE

PLEASURABLE OR OTHERWISE, an overnight stay at Corrour is always a memorable experience.

> The Corrour Bothy was our objective. On drawing near, we noticed smoke coming from the chimney, and peering in at the window saw a man apparently asleep, lying full length on the floor before a blazing log fire. As we entered, the man arose and with becoming dignity said: 'Good morning, gentlemen, I have a good fire ready for you.' For this we heartily thanked him. While our outer garments were drying, we had a substantial breakfast and a long rest, cause by the rain-storm which did not abate till afternoon.
>
> Henry C. Dugan, 'A Midnight Experience at the Derry',
> CCJ No 71, 1926

> There were nine men in Corrour
> Who arrived from all parts of the moor.
> Said the dog with delight
> There are no more in sight,
> But I wish the hell there were fewer.
>
> 23 September 1928

> Arrived at 8.30pm in a torrent of rain. After oozing from our garments to the melodious moan of the Primus as it cooked our supper – sizzling bacon etc… We slept the sleep of satiation after a hectic game of bezique.
>
> 16 July 1929

The much-loved Primus stove was the first pressurised-burner paraffin stove. Others followed in its wake, but the Primus had a reputation for reliability and was universally used in the UK. It even accompanied the successful 1953 Everest expedition.

Now sitting with belts slackened after a skirl of beans, tea, bread
etc – a real tightener… There seems to be less furniture around this
year – burned I suppose. As there are but 20 cards left… we look
like having a dull evening.

M Mitchell, 31 May 1931

I hope 'Eko' embrocation is a good blanket as it's the only one I have.
It heats up well if spread on ginger biscuits.

10 June 1931

The 'Barron couple' are not yet up – 10.30am. Perfect disgrace! The
way some people take things easy!!! But I wish I was still in bed too.

11 Jun 1931

The Barron couple reply…

The 'Barron couple' are taking it easy. The cold weather convinces us
that we would be warmer in the sleeping bags than out of them.

11 Jun 1931

Picture four semi-naked madmen, and the arrival of two sprightly
damsels (with partners). This condition due to (in our inadequately
clothed bodies) the inclemency of these abominable hills. Having fed,
and the embarrassing element away, we feel considerably better apart
from the fact that I, the writer, have meanwhile no trousers and no
shoes. Washing calls me so I must needs stop these ramblings.

Marcus FH Greenhorne, 19 July 1931

Tramped up Carn Ban Mor till 10.30pm and pitched tent in bog.
Had to be bog or water. Slept in said bog or lay in bog till 7am.
Returned to Corrour absolutely pulped. Peat like a sieve and boots
pulped. Bert burst his shoe and had to descend to Corrour with
one foot in a spare rucksack. This bothy is like the Savoy Hotel.
12 in bothy but number decreasing. Varied aromas from socks and
tomatoes all cooking & eating. Probably leaving tomorrow for Luibeg.
Weather improving but ground like a morass. Trews and kilt soaking.
Everything absolutely swamped. Bert is frying some 'pommes de terre
à la Cairngorms'.

Edward C Malcolm, 20 July 1931

Arrived at 8pm yesterday from Aberdeen. Meant to climb Braeriach but decided not to when we saw the weather. Had a good night. Fyfe has left half-crowns all over the place, as he spilt his cash on the floor last night.

SA Middleton, 9 August 1931

The three lads have now returned. Two of them are preparing to go bathing in the Dee (9.15pm). Enthusiasm is a good thing, but for me enthusiasm does not manifest itself in such feats of endurance as plunging into icy waters at dusk on a chill May evening – good luck to them.

Paul J Peace, 16 May 1937

Ken is producing weird noises from a much battered mouth organ and prides himself that he is making music. I hate to disillusion him but am afraid I must, with an edge-nailed boot.

R Manning, 5 July 1937

We have been making a very thorough scientific investigation of the peat bog and my colleagues inform me that the nature of the peat in the bog is excellent and if dried would be an excellent antidote to draughts. So we would make a humble suggestion that those who come up after May, June or July should cut some peats and lay them out to dry somewhere near the bothy and leave instructions for those who follow to gather them in.

Norman MacDonald, 7 April 1938

Had a long lie (well-earned). Got up 2.20pm. Washed four days' dishes. Tidied bothy with a woman's touch. Made good fire. Finished the day with sing-song round the fire. What singing!

Jimmy, 20 July 1938

It is the most comfortable Temperance Hotel at which I have ever stopped. It is equipped with a tin opener of modern design and its selection of Primus prickers is second to none. All home comforts are provided and appreciated. I am proposing to bequeath it my kettle.

KA Gray, 16 June 1939

A pricker was required to clean the jet of the Primus stove.

The following is an extract from a detailed account of a stay at Corrour that runs to five detailed visitors' book pages.

By 9pm the Devil's Point was in view and then the bothy. Wishful thinking made me see smoke curling from the bothy but having waded the burn in stocking soles I made my way up to find the door barred. The time was about 9.45pm, which I'm thinking wasn't so bad for a mere woman on a lonesome trail. I'd carted with me from a good 2 miles back the way a log weather-worn and grey.

Having dried my shivering feet I got out dry shoes and set about something to eat, for though I'd picked up a bargain in bananas at the van in Inverey – two bananas in one skin – I'd had nothing to eat since 4 o'clock. Thereafter I tried to sleep – flannel pyjamas above a skirt – tweed – jacket of the same said but on beneath costume jacket – waterproof buttoned close to hide the motley array lest I should have a late visitor and with shorts wrapped around my toes. I lay down to sleep hoping to wake to a new day – refreshed and ready for the trail.

At about 12.15am I got up, lit a match and took the log, which was hissing and beautifully warm, to 'bed' with me. Even such a novel bedwarmer didn't do the trick, however, and here I am wasting valuable heat setting my log into life by feeding it all the available heather. Where's daylight – and more important – the sunshine to completely suffuse me with warmth? (shades of my school teaching, I've split my infinitive back there). I'll feel just fine – at the moment I'm wondering why the Hades I ever left my comfortable digs in Ballater, where I could have been content for another couple of days walking around Muick and Lochnagar. Brainwave. Ralph Bates' 'Fear Him' is in my rucksack. I bought it in Banchory on Tuesday to while away the time on the bus. For the nonce, au revoir.

6.30 the following morning:

After a sleepless night I feel I could feel fit for Aviemore if only it would stop raining. I kept up as good a fire as I could all night but couldn't read – no concentration about 2 o'clock. I began to see the funny side of the business and by 3 I was sitting, having a laugh all on my own. I had a look out about 3 to make sure it was daylight I was seeing and

by 4 o'clock it was greying with dawn. At precisely 20 minutes 05,
ie 4.40, I heard the first mountain crakes give voice in their clucking
throats. At about 5 I decided that if the rain would clear off a fraction
I would collect my odds & ends and make for Aviemore. Now at 6.45
the rain is pouring harder than ever. If it carries on like this I'll never
make Aviemore.

Had only one scare during the night. The fire was blazing merrily –
lighting up even the furthest corners – when the sharp rat-tat of
steps on stones came to my ears for a minute. I sat tense in a sweat
wondering what the blazes? I laughed at myself and realised it must
be deer.

(By the way, I write in red ink italics only because of my badge
of office – namely my marking pen, which happens to be my only
one here.)

My socks are now dry (I washed them while I cooked breakfast).
I think I'll damn the rain and go ahead with preparations for being off.
If F.S.A.F. passes this way and reads and sighs at my effusiveness, let him
please to remember I am <u>alone</u>!

Lilian M Cameron, MA, 9 August 1940

Last night was the weirdest I've spent here. We retired at 12.30 and,
being unable to sleep, four of the eight on the floor regaled each
other with such poems as they could remember. They varied from
The Shooting of Dan McGrew to The Lady of Shalott. Meanwhile
Fearlas Mor rattled the bothy door and stars twinkled through a hole
in the roof, the moon meanwhile fitfully illuminating the fireplace.
Eventually I rocked the others to sleep with La Belle Dame Sans
Merci and was left in the ignominious position of being left awake
when the others were asleep. I must have dropped off about 4.00am.
And now for civilisation.

N Rosenblatt, 18 August 1940

Out of paraffin. Suffocated by heather fire smoke. Going to Braemar
for supplies.

K King, 6 April 1950

Took tip from previous entries and after much digging removed large
tree root from nearby bog – it nearly burned.

RA Jeffrey, 21 May 1950

Next time I shall bring a sleeping bag.

G Worsley, 13 August 1950

The 'brown heath' makes a wonderful bed — but be careful to smooth out
the 'craggy wood' bits before settling down for the night.

KW Paul, 13 August 1950

Abandoned all attempts to walk across the bridge and paddled across
instead. Rather wearing on the feet! Spent quite a comfortable night
in the company of three mad Scots and two mad Australians. The
men say they couldn't sleep because there were four women v only
three of them. We are all speaking to each other this morning. Were
lulled to sleep by one mad Scot making an imperial din on their
mouth organ and singing crude songs. Two stags came down to greet
us this morning.

Barbara Usher, 5 September 1952

One member of the party established the record for shaving before
going to bed, to please the lady who slept beside him — he even
wore pyjamas!! One of the young ladies went out to wash and lost
her front suspension in the river. Our convert from sixth-grade
rock climbing wore a ladies bathing cap to keep his hair dry and our
fairy-footed schoolteacher a Grenfell jacket and a pair of shorts like a
Greek ballet skirt.

Philip Scott, 17 July 1953

Having spent two nights recently on my own at the Ryvoan Bothy
and the Shelter Stone, it was a pleasant (?) change to spend the
night at Corrour in the company of seven men, five women and a
pigeon. There was plenty of room for all rucksacks included and
the party were all settled down by 11.00pm. Peace reigned until
11.55pm when it was shattered by someone asking was it time
for breakfast yet. This led to a general uproar, flashing of torches,
the lighting of a candle and then a general sing-song. There was
then a further period of silence until about 3.00am when a girl's
voice enquired about the whereabouts of the frying pan. Uproar
again ensued. A bright and cheery party arose at 4.30am to
prepare breakfast.

William A Cooke, 14 June 1954

Arrived thankfully on Tuesday near 1800 hours. Had travelled
from Aviemore since Sunday with progress very slow since wife
and I heavily laden with rucksacks of 7 days' rations and our young
child of 2 years 7 months who only periodically walks, so one can
imagine our task over the rock- and boulder-laden pass by the Pools
of Dee. Were compelled to camp at the Pools (Monday night),
where a camping site is more precious than gold, as time was then
2200 hours.

Weather remained, Tuesday and Wednesday, overcast with low
clouds, therefore a thankful rest of recuperation all Wednesday,
during which two pairs of campers paid a visit when they prepared
their lunch. In the evenings neighbouring deer came quite close and
as many as nine were visible.

Thursday morning a strong wind cleared the threatening clouds,
giving us a sunny blue sky and revealing the splendour of the lofty
peaks and Glen Dee. 12.30pm. We bid farewell to our home, the
thankful haven of Corrour Bothy.

Mr and Mrs PW Anderson and child, 15 June 1954

The Dundee Rucksack Club distinguished themselves in the hut
purely by example in that they caused a GUM Club party to keep
quiet and go to bed before 11 o'clock each night. This made a
good impression on the GUM Club, so much so that when the
Rucksack Club left, the GUM Club only stayed up until 1am the
next night.

20 March 1955

The GUM Club (Glasgow University Mountaineering Club)
and Dundee University Rucksack Club always had a vigorous
rivalry.

From our Corrour fashion correspondent:

[A party of seven from Gordonstoun School set off for Cairn
Toul and Braeriach.] One of the party returned rather demoralised
by plague, beri beri or some such malady, accompanied by two
others as a means of safe conduct to Luibeg and R. Scott esq (whom
God preserve). These safe conductors are worthy of mention, the
larger of the two because he burnt stewed apples to an unparalleled
degree in my canteen, and the other because of the hue of his

clothing – pillar-box red socks, almond green corduroy trousers and a
very blue pullover.

Les Weatherall, 7 June 1955

We arrived Corrour 30th, spent the night here then left for a party
at Aviemore (6hr) on 31st. We returned in the wee sma' hours of
1st, arriving here 10.30am after a rather wet journey back. The party
in the Cairngorm Hotel was most enjoyable and well worth the
double journey.

James Fyfe & James Hunter, 1 January 1956

This regal erection, designed for the comfort and wellbeing of
enlightened people who scale mountains for pleasure, was blessed
with my presence on 23rd & 24th September 1956. Already at
the mansion, living like pampered lads, were eleven other well-
educated fools. The company was magnificent. Filthy jokes were
left hanging in the bright blue air with an abandon that bore
evidence of the gaiety of their characters. They were all fit, cheerful,
fine fellows.

Andrew Allan, 24 September 1956

Arrived from Aviemore. Slept in polythene wardrobe bags.
An experience never to be repeated. Emptied the dew out in the
morning. Went up the east ridge to take off the stiffness. Left after
dinner for Braemar. Leaving tinned food for you. Enjoy them.

Pat Butcher, 7 August 1959

Arrived here after a very hard walk from Braemar... hard and heavy
rain making the path like a river. Being somewhat damp I lit a fire with
pencil shavings, paper and the heather from the floor as there was
no wood around... I found this book looking rather lonely so I made
friends with it and proceeded to read. I would like to thank all who
wrote in it before me for it made my evening cheery, for I am alone
here (haven't saw the mouse yet). I needed such as this.

Please note that even though the sea strike is on I do not support
it for I prefer the trials and troubles of my mountains and hills than
tho's of the sea. Well, I'll smoke my cigarette now and retire to
bunk. Goodnight.

Peter Japp, Merchant Navy, 28 June 1966

The 1966 seaman's strike over working hours caused so much disruption that the government declared a state of emergency.

After two minutes' camping on the opposite shore last night, we decided the 'healthy life' was not for us. The ten of us spent the night here sucking each other's socks and counting the lice. Two gallant members stayed on the other side (the smell here being overpowering) and sailed down to Aberdeen on the morning tide.

A Venables, 14 August 1966

In order to alleviate the boredom caused by inclement weather, sore feet and other excuses for doing nothing but festering in the bothy, I have founded Corrour Bothy Library with book number 1 *The Passionflower Hotel* by Rosalind Erskine. If all the patrons of this bothy donated one paperback or even a magazine, the library would become a special attraction on its own, provided that nobody decides to walk off with books, as happened at St Valery refuge. The possibilities for the bothy's future development are endless. When I come back from the Far East in 1970 I look forward to seeing piles of books, art displays, flower gardens, miniature zoo and a strip joint.

John M Patchett, Normandy Company, Sandhurst, 24 August 1966

Dry heather burns well & warms bothy in a few minutes. Any green in it will smoke the place out!

Hamish Brown, 5 November 1969

Sound advice from Hamish, the first person to walk all the Munros in a single trip.

Downie family arrived for a night's sleep out of the howling wind. As the day wore on we were ten to the floor and little Shona (7) roared 'Roll over'.

18 July 1979

Dear Reader
    Since the majority of people who read this are going to stay the night, we'd better say something nice to stop you getting too depressed.

Firstly, the flat parts of the floor are exceedingly comfy and the smoke, which doesn't go up the chimney, is very warm and comforting when you're frightened out of your mind by the intrepid 'bigfoot' which haunts Ben Macdui and this bothy alternately.

Secondly, the rodents and reptiles that frequent this bothy are very friendly indeed providing you give them enough food. If you don't, they are always ready to make a healthy meal out of your toes as you lie sleeping.

I trust you will find this information helpful.

17 October 1979

Wish I could get a fire going. There's only a bit if charred log here and I think that's made of asbestos.

10 March 1982

In 1996, 'Hugh and Liz' chose Corrour as a base for three days to celebrate their wedding. They arrived with accompanying wedding party, coal for the fire and much food and drink. The visitors' book contains six pages of goodwill messages. A good time was had by all, including surprised passers-by.

Wonderful wedding breakfast. (Mike and Sandra)
    We have wined and dined like kings and queens. (Sue Walsh)
    Came for solitude, ended up in a wedding reception.
Great company.
    Have a whisky, they said. Sorted, says I. Smashing surprise. (David Huston)
    On the way to Cairn Toul and heard of a wedding. So popped in for a celebratory dram. (Lesley King)

3–5 May 1996

Tonight Corrour Bothy had the proud honour of hosting the national plastic rustling competition of 1998. The winners, with non stop-plastic rustling until 4.30am, were the Scotland/Essex group. Exhausted by their neighbours' nocturnal activities, the team from Kent were forced to sleep in until 8.30. Essex/Scotland meantime had gone for their climb of the Angel's Peak, forced into action by impending hypothermia – they

had brought no sleeping bags! The proud team now go forward to
the world championships to be held on the Everest Base Camp route
in October.

Andy, 26 June 1998

Dear Sir/Madam, we the undersigned are grateful to the warm heart
of the Corrour Bothy and its convivial guests. A splendid ceilidh was
had with a full set for Virginia Reel and couples taking to the floor for
St Bernard's Walk. Poetry, tall tales and an evening conquest of the
Devil's Point. We returned to the huge French culinary delights of
butter and fresh garlic.

Robin, Ottilie, Anna, Elizabeth, Robin, Nic, Basia, Karen,
19 May 2019

BOTHY CUISINE

AFTER A LONG DAY in the wilds, <u>any</u> meal can seem like a king's banquet... or maybe not.

No sunshine falls on the bothy walls,
Nought but the wind and rain,
But our spirits soar as the Primi roar,
For we'll soon have dinner again.

Alexander B Donald, 6 August 1928

If you are making a stay of more than three days at Corrour, you will not likely be able to carry enough food to do your whole holiday, and a day must be spent going to Aviemore or Braemar. It is approximately 15 miles to either. Braemar is preferable, as it is an easier walk and better shopping centre. If you go by Braemar in the first instance, it is possible to have arrangements made whereby provisions will be left for you at Linn of Dee and this takes 16 miles off your journey.

'A Bothy Holiday in the Hills', Dundee Courier,
17 August 1929

Great tragedy occurred today. A huge frying pan full of bacon and baked beans hurtled to the floor amid curses, oaths, swears, imprecations and other tokens of supreme disapproval. Oh! What a fall was here, my countrymen.

8 July 1931

Glad to get out of the rain. The grub's already running low owing to the great capacity of my friend here. I have never travelled with him before.

W Henry, 4 August 1937

We crossed the stones at the infant Dee
Then brewed ourselves a cup of tea
But alas the milk was lacking
However we drank it and then went packing.

EM Metcalfe, 8 August 1937

Supply your own follow-up story to this next visitors' simple but cryptic record.

HAVE PUT KETTLE ON TO BOIL

23 July 1939

Time on our hands led to experiments in cooking. Hit on the following recipe:
    Half tin corned beef
    Half tin baked beans (small)
Mash up well together. Add quarter cup water with third cup Oxo. Add oatmeal until fairly stiff and fry the whole damned issue in plenty of fat. Then dig a hole at a safe distance from the bothy and bury the lot.

A Gill, 8 August 1939

Today the weather is b----- awful. Tried various recipes including flapjacks (which we contemplated soling our shoes with)… More experiments in cooking – chocolate cake and plum duff. 'Baking mode' in stove turned out to be 'wishing mode' – now don't say we didn't tell you. Experiments hardly successful.

8 August 1939

Christmas Day 1939 saw the first existing entry in the visitors' books by a female member of a climbing club and the first recorded winter visit by a woman. The Pinnacle Club is a women's climbing club formed in 1921. Phyllis White joined in 1936 and was obviously an enthusiastic member.

Arrived from the Shelter Stone via Cairn Gorm in the night… Fortunately there was a very good moon for travelling, although the snow is thawing (a westerly gale). We had a marvellous dinner consisting of a rum aperitif – pemmican soup, savoury black pudding – a Xmas cake – tea – Xmas pudding soaked in rum – & Ovaltine. Finishing off with a rum nightcap. Unfortunately we were not able to eat all the Xmas pudding so we have bequeathed it to the next inhabitants.

Phyllis B. White (Pinnacle Club), with three male colleagues,
25 December 1939

[After three days of resting] This as you will notice is another of my bad days. I rose early and due to lack of bread had to go into Inverey and, after cadging, secured two loaves (20 miles).
William Rodger, 22 July 1940

Rations for two persons for five days:

4 loaves, ½lb flour, 1½lb sugar, 1 large tin milk, 1lb jam, ½lb onions, 1lb semolina, ¼lb tea, 1 dozen Oxos, ½lb dripping, ½lb butter, 1 dozen eggs, 1lb cheese, 1 bottle coffee, 2oz cocoa
August 1940

Arrived in a raging snowstorm. Had no food so went out and shot a tin of bully, which we saw lurking in a bog. When we dragged it back, found it was bad so had to boil some of our boots, which we decided by cutting the cards. This we boiled (the boot not the cards) and cut into three parts, one having the sole, one the uppers, and the heel and toe cap and laces to the other. Very cold, fingers frozen. Long live Scotland.
Signed: Three Musketeers, 24 June 1943

We left a bottle of whisky on top of Ben MacDhui. Don't strain yourself on the way up.
Ian Robertson, 3 October 1948.

HERE WE ARE BACK AT CORROUR,
WEATHER VERY DULL.
WE HAVE JUST HAD A FEED,
AND NOW FEEL VERY FULL.

6 June 1949

RECIPE FOR PAN OAT CAKES –

MEAL (any amount), FLOUR (any amount), SALT (none), MILK (none), WATER (plenty in burn), mix any way, fry, take out when burned – result: ?X)</>! (curse).

15 August 1950

Periodic blizzards all day. Water hole under 5ft of snow. Evolved a new dish. Boil macaroni until glutinous. Add cheese and underdone onions. Boil again and throw away. Ended a rather disastrous day by burning a pair of socks.

19 May 1951

Left Braemar after discovering the butchers were closed, thus depriving me of yet another opportunity of buying meat. However, luncheon meat and beans saved the day (together with a drop of soup).

Alan Price, 4 September 1951

Tea, Porage, Bacon & Luncheon Meat, Porage, Tea. No paraffin. Delete 2nd tea.

6 September 1951

Dearly beloved brethren
    It is not a sin
To eat a raw potato
    And throw away the skin.
Let the sin feed the stags
    And the stags feed you
Dearly beloved brethren
    Is this not true?

Written in classical Alexandrine hexameters, being originally translated from the Greek by the Spanish critic Cervantes.

CR Robert, 19 July 1955

Very weary but plenty of beery.
Not so frisky but still some whisky.

26 September 1959

Festered all morning since snow was very soft. We found a tin of
compo rations outside the bothy and had it with rice and Pan Yan
pickle for dinner – magnificent. We went up Devil's Point, Angel's
Peak and Cairn Toul this afternoon and returned soaked. We have
already retired to the sweaty depths of our respective flea-bags and
we now bid you a cheery goodnight.

Eric Henry, 5 April 1966

Compo (composite) rations are canned, dried and pre-packaged
meals used by the military for minimal preparation in the field.
Pan Yan was a spicy pickle produced from 1923–2002.

The chef recommends: Hanche de Venison Rôti
    Trim off a haunch of venison by removing chine bone and the
end of the knuckle. Wrap well in greased paper to prevent fat from
burning. Roast for 2½–3 hours, basting frequently. Remove from
paper and brush with butter to colour a good brown. Dredge lightly
with flour and continue to baste until it is well covered. Make a gravy
with the residue from the pan, plus any trimmings. Serve redcurrant
jelly separately. Suggestion: may also be served avec chestnut purée.
    PS Venison should be hung for at least six days before use (not in
the bothy, please!).
    PPS Catch your deer first!!

28 May 1966

Recipe for first meal

1st course: 1 pkt of soup to gallon of water
Comment: tasted like monkey's p---
2nd course: Mashed beefburgers & beans & dumpling things
Comment: Delicious, very tasty and satisfying

…

Tried to light fire but failed. Used up paraffin. Finally succeeded by
pouring Glaxo & sugar on logs and placing Primus under fireplace.
    Short nap from 4pm to 6pm then tea, mince and tatties. Lay in
sleeping bags till 10.00pm then lights out. Kept awake by howling
wind and stampeding shrews.

Breakfast at 10am. Mushroom omelette, bacon and
fried mushrooms.
11.15am Off to Devil's Point.

31 October 1970

Swapped can of macaroni cheese, value about 20p, for 2 packets of
dehydrated savoury fry, value 76p. We thought we were the ones
getting a good deal. Wrong. Pity the person who eats savoury fry
unless he wants to commit suicide.

A Hogarth, 20 August 1977

It's now half past four and we've been eating since 9 this morning,
the last effort being Ian's speciality – 3 pints water, 2 packets Instant
Whip (chocolate), 1 Kitkat, 3 crumbled Ryvitas, 1 glurp of marge,
soggy powdered milk, nuts and raisins… and Sally insisted on the
pepper (optional).

30 June 1980

I certainly recommend some of the blue cheese I found under
the table.

Jerome (Gibraltar), 26 May 1996

I don't know about you, but I can't stand dehydrated food and Raven's
Hot Cereal Start did nothing to change my mind. And they have the
cheek to write 'Bon Appetit' on the packet.

Antony Wiles, 1 July 1997

No longer available and not to be confused with other brand
names or products, Hot Cereal Start was an add-hot-water wheat-
based breakfast cereal. Antony's entirely subjective review of the
confection should be weighed against the far more objective reviews
of those of us who have fond memories of it as a lightweight, tasty
and nourishing breakfast on extended backpacking trips.

In the very words of a certain Mr R. Burns, 'Only man's mind could
have mapped into abstraction such a territory'. These words I could
well agree with, having taken in the view from the top of Ben Macdui.
However! My day was horribly spoiled by experiencing the devil's
broth that is BEANFEAST. Please, please, please, please heed the

above warning and consign the satanic stew of genetic skulduggery to
the very depths from where it came.

Rich, 7 July 1998

Glorious sunshine. Found some wild mushrooms (chanterelles,
ceps & sparassis) and put juniper berries in the stew. Heather in
bloom – lovely.

Laurence, 2 September 1998

BEASTIES AND GHOSTIES
MIDGIES

CULICOIDES IMPUNCTATUS IS a local resident whose over-enthusiastic welcome to Corrour's summer visitors is not always universally appreciated.

Beautiful weather – when the sun comes out you are pestered by flies, and when it goes in you are bitten to death by midges.

A Gibb, 7 August 1939

Fed well despite the look of the food we cooked. Midges also fed well every time we ventured out.

9 August 1939

Midges Midges Everywhere

J Mitchell, 1 August 1952

Slogged up from Inverey in 90°F sun feeling rather like a camel with an outsized hump. Smelt this place before I saw it and after enduring the gnats for two or three hours decided to enjoy the comparative luxury of a night on Devil's Point. Today after enduring the gnats for four or five hours have decided to enjoy the comparative luxury of a night on Ben Macdhui.

4 August 1957

In the true tradition of the nature reserve, we gave protection to approximately 50% of Scotland's midges last night.

18 August 1966

Bothy became overcrowded so spent night trying out a new tent. Awoke to revolting sight of millions of midges using tent as landing base. Returned rapidly to bothy.

David G Longstaff, July 31, 1972

143

Far across the swamp of despair,
Deep down in the darkest cleft,
Or buried in the thickest heather,
A terror lies in wait for the flesh of men,
Its teeth are sharp, it sucks blood freely,
This new fear they call the midge.

14 August 1984

We should eradicate them all – every last one of them. Kill them
when they sleep, kill them when they eat, kill them when they mate.
I hate sodding midges.

Kenny Richmont, 26 August 1996

We love the Scottish midges – we love them when they're dead!

14 August 1997

MICE

GENERATIONS OF BOTHY mice have been immortalised in the visitors' books, eliciting entries both charitable and otherwise.

We did intend to sleep in the bothy but an excess of rodent life therein necessitated pitching camp outside. We arrived at about 3.30 to be duly welcomed by the 'hütte vater' [*Alpine hut guardian*], Mr Mouse and Mrs Beetle, who had evidently been spending their time in the larder instead of keeping the hut clean.

W Gordon Graham, 22 June 1938

Spent a comfortable night here. The bothy mouse is certainly no myth. After introducing itself to us yesterday, its friendliness developed into familiarity and it spent the night at the foot of one of our sleeping bags until ejected the next morning.

GY Stoddart, 29 August 1939

Some say to kill the bothy mouse,
Some say to let it be
But Burns alone is abune a',
He let his mouse go free.

WM Duguid, 15 July 1940

Please leave a Christmas dinner for the mice. They are very friendly.

Farid Ahmed, 25 December 1952

Last night a horrifying tragedy occurred – (Ken) Grassick sat on one of the mice and killed it. Its piteously flattened body was cremated in the fireplace.

A Graham Nicol, 30 December 1952

145

Ode to a Mountain Mouse (with apologies to Robert Burns)

Wee sleekit, cowrin', timorous beastie,
O what a panic's in thy breastie,
We canna come to run and chase thee,
We've got to go,
Besides we've baith got muckle blisters
On heel and toe.

James Dunlop, 23 July 1959

May we introduce the quietest member of our party – MR MOUSE.
It seems he has opted to spend the winter alone in the confines of
Corrour. If you see him, please try to cheer him up with a few titbits
of you-know-what and make him welcome. PS He likes empty tin cans,
which he pushes round the bothy all night.

Tony Bellhouse, Rucksack Club, 27 November 1965

Oh Corrour, Corrour, what a welcome sight,
A place wherein to spend the night.
After the last two miles of fighting for breath,
And doing our best to ward off death,
You offer us shelter and, for free,
A mouse with whom to share our tea!

Written at the sign of the frozen sock by DG Powell,
16 April 1966

Walked up from Aviemore YH carrying about 70lbs apiece – a thing to
be done but not repeated. 12 miles took 8½ hours. Hope the mouse
is a mythical beast – one chewed through my tent last week and we
ended up chasing it with a piton hammer at 3am!

Martin Hogg, 1 June 1966

Walked up from Derry Lodge last night with Susan to get away from
the others, who camped at Derry. The mouse paid us his nocturnal
visit but didn't trundle any cans on this occasion. He merely walked
about in what must have been heavy climbing boots and loudly
ate polythene.

21 May 1966

You will be pleased to know that the mouse is alive and well, which
is not surprising considering the amount of our food that he eats. He
also seems to have been provided with 'bovver' boots, with which he
tramps over us in the night. [*The following day*] The mouse had a hungry
night last night as we hung all the food from the ceiling, but we are
leaving him some bacon fat and Quaker oats.

Robin Thomas, 25 February 1971

My glasses were broken last night by a rampaging field mouse now lying
half-dead in the fireplace because Richards won't give it the kiss of life.

23 June 1971

Them mice get everywhere. I must be one of the few people who
don't mind mice running over the faces but these b-----s shout in
your ear to make sure you're awake and then do a sand dance on the
polythene sheet. All very spooky when you're on your own close to
Fearlas Mor haunts.

Jim Craigon, 10 May 1972

Spent miserable night due to cold discomfort and mice, millions
of them. One of us strangely attacked by a vicious mouse at 1am.
Narrowly escaped with his sandwiches. Driven out onto the hillside
finally at 3.40am after estimated 1½ hours sleep in 7 hours.

DJ Boam, 29 June 1972

I was welcomed by the two bothy mice on arrival. They just popped
in to see who it was and did I have an Alpen? They seem very tame.
Perhaps they are employed by the MBA as custodians.

Robin MacLean, 5 October 1977

Mice have been eating the batteries, but they got a shock.

5 October 1977

Arrived late last night after walking non-stop for 9 days. We were low
on food and water, but morale was surprisingly cheerful. One of our
group perished after being eaten by a gang of field mice. We buried
him on top of Cairn Gorm. It was a simple funeral.

7 July 1996

Methinks the mouse could be a possum or even a koala, judging by
the noise it makes in the wee small hours.

Fergus Madigan (Australia), 13 September 1997

The mouse likes cheese.

Richard, 13 June 1998

Didn't have a problem with the mouse last night (I slept outside).

Methalda, 29 July 1998

Mouse made it outside to tent – likes porridge oats.

Kenneth McKnight, 9 September 1998

I had the place to myself, except for the resident field mice, who
were more than a little nuisance. As soon as the light started to fade
and I had entered my sleeping bag, they emerged noisily from the
fireplace and started to run about the floor. If I kept motionless they
would cheekily stand on their hind legs about a foot from my face.
With their huge ears and oversized whiskers they really are cute, but
the idea of them actually invading my person kept me awake until
I resorted to semi-suffocation in an almost totally enclosed bag. The
combination of mice-induced insomnia and the concrete floor made
getting up next morning unusually pleasant.

Jack Connell, 'A Walk Across Scotland', ccj 105, June 1999

OTHER BEASTIES

MICE AND MIDGES aren't the only wildlife encountered at Corrour.

Bothy surrounded by 'mooing' deer during the night – like a farm yard.

3 September 1929

Obviously written by a confused naturalist.

Having spent a glorious night scratching ourselves, we got up at 7am. Heard the roaring of stags through the night. At first we thought it was the spectre of Ben Macdui. Then Bill confirmed his stomach was out of order. The stags sounded more like a baritone tomcat doing the 'Feline Nocturne'.

E Rothney, 29 August 1931

A few coveys of ptarmigan bolting about. Why are the birds so tame? Why do they prefer to walk rather than fly from us? And what do they feed so high for?

7 January 1936

The deer are still belling.

4 October 1936

This is the correct term for a deer's call.

Saw a large male [deer] sunning itself. It looked as though it had had a very good meal and wouldn't do anything except blink its eyes when poked with a stick.

22 July 1937

NB Poking a stag with any kind of implement is neither commendable nor prudent.

The stags are now barking incessantly, sometimes right outside the bothy. I had fun watching and photographing a stag which was less than 25 feet from the door.

Jack Scroggie, 30 September 1939

Well, at least they're not mooing.

It was a glorious day. We saw no one the whole day and the only incident worth noting was the finding of a ptarmigan's nest. We were anxious to see if there were eggs in the nest but the bird sat close and allowed us to stroke her & eventually had to be pushed off, disclosing several eggs. She only moved a couple of yards and was back on the nest before we were well away.

Winnie Morrison, 4 June 1942

All wildlife should of course be left undisturbed, with the possible exception of midges and intruders—

Distressed pigeon on window sill. However, it will not let me touch it, neither will it eat food offered.

29 August 1950

It was still there three days later.

On returning to bothy about 3pm, found the 'Poor Doo' apparently moribund. The doo has since had a second lease of life and is now busily engaged in disposing of the midges (or something) which are apparently bothering him/her.

PR Wycherley, 1 September 1950

It was still there a fortnight later.

The pigeon is still here. I gave it some corned beef and porridge and it passed into an ecstatic coma.

David Alasdair McNaughton (Cardiff Medical College),
13 September 1950

After an ascent of The Chimney, Corrour Bothy, we set off for the high peaks. A pair of dotterel and a single downy 'younk' were observed on the Braeriach plateau.

RM Preshaw, 11 July 1951

Younk is Scots for a young bird.

Localised winds of hurricane force. Last night kept awake by stag
rummaging on tin heap.

Alan Ramsbottom, 6 June 1955

God bless the builder of this shelter! Dying for a kip. Watch out for
snakes. I just missed one by 3 inches!

Gogsie Watson, 2 May 1972

My name is Sharon Blyth and I am 13 years old. My young brother
caught a real creepy wee frog and it was jumping about as if it had
ants in its pants or up here it would be midges.

Sharon Blyth, 6 August 1977

Flurries of snow in the night. Visits from the gusting wind and the
bothy mouse (at least I hope it was only a mouse). Pied wagtails,
deer on the mountain, ptarmigan still partly in winter feathers,
and the solitude of the mountains – our mountains – all lovely
memory makers.

Joyce, 11 May 1996

Just stopping for 15mins to get out of the sun. Surveying for water
vole populations above the Dee. So far – lots of signs of water voles
all around the tributaries, so watch your step. The Cairngorms may
be the last stronghold for the UK's most/fastest disappearing mammal.
If you see one, savour the view!

Ian Fazey, 12 August 1997

Captain's Log Supplemental. Air uninhabitable. Ground soft. Weird alien
on 4 legs walked past the door. Midges fatal. Beam me up Scotty.

Captain James. T Kirk, aka Simon Holden, June 18, 1998

Overnighting by bothy. Despite smell of wine, 3 beautiful stags
wandered/grazed by us for near 2 hours. Spectacular animals,
scenery & weather. PS Went for a walk, upon return found a family
of 12 deer grazing – one foal, a few yearlings still losing their winter
coat. Cool!!!

W John (Australia), 9 July 1998

GHOSTIES

IN THE LONELY outpost of Corrour, imagination can run as wild as the surroundings.

For Ghoulies and ghosties
And four-legged beasties
And things that go bump in the night
Good Lord deliver us.

13 September 1928

One of the boys woke up during the night and thought he saw the Corrour ghost, but investigation proved it only to be a luminous haddy.

Walter Winchell, 1 January 1936

A haddy is a haddock or a pejorative term for an Aberdonian. Make of this what you will.

Beware of ghosts. Last night we were locked in and couldn't get out. The swivel locking bar on the outside of the door had for some curious fashion locked on its own – we were locked in – we poked with a knife for ½hour until we successfully removed the bar from its hold. Beware.

16 August 1936

A party of honest men sat up all night, reciting incantations, breathing mystic profanities and creating a ghostly atmosphere, but no ghosts appeared. Bottled spirits alone were in evidence but alas! they too are gone and nothing remains but crapulence and scepticism.

Cairngorm Ghosts, 2 January 1937

I was chased by a bogey all the way from the highest summit of
Braeriach down to the Lairig where I think it lost me among the
boulders. It was a horrid grey thing and it really made me frightened.
I am serious and shivering with fright.

25 July 1955

Tales of the spectre Fearlas Mor (The Big Grey Man of Ben Macdui) are legion. Eminent Victorian Alpinist Norman Collie related
(in jest?) how he fled the summit in panic when he heard giant
footsteps behind him.

Fascinated by the Lairig 6 years ago. Decided to have another
look... I also came this way to trace the Grey Man, or at least to
hear his famed footsteps. Late last night, just as I dozed off, there
were the steps – and they stopped outside the bothy. 'That's him,'
I thought. The door handle creaked – the door opened – and there
was not one grey man but two of them – Inverey hikers. Is there a
Grey Man?

Michael Corper, 6 August 1955

One of the two 'grey men' has added 'Bloody Cheek!'

The mist was swirling close at hand,
The candle flickered in its stand,
When the Big Grey Man came down the Ben,
Seeking his supper – two Yorkshire men.
He shook the roof, he brayed on t' door,
But there they cooked on the bothy floor
(Unperturbed by Fearlas Mor).
At last they opened up with caution,
And palmed him off with a fish portion.

P Daynes, 20 September 1957

Just passing through...

The Grey Man, 15 September 1958

This morning early we climbed Macdui,
There was nae Grey Man (the story's hooey)

18 September 1958

Left Aberdeen 1810 Thursday night and walked up as far as this
side of the Lui bridge. Spent a rather uncomfortable night owing to
what I swear were breathing noises. (I was alone and it wasn't me
I was hearing.) They were definitely inhaling and exhaling noises so
I'm pretty sure it was neither the wind nor the sound of the burn.
Anyway, got up at first light and couldn't find any signs of it having
been a deer, so maybe the Grey Man of Macdui was out for a stroll
and got lost.

Neil Reid, 27 May 1977

Were woken up about midnight by strange thumping noises outside.
I had been regaling my partner with stories about Baird and Barrie,
who died around here in 1928... Anyway, for peace of mind we
decided the noises were deer grazing but it's the last time I'll spend a
night here.

Mark Cullen, 24 June 1979

Got here about 7.30pm. Bedded down 9pm. Got a visitor about
midnight – the Big Grey Man of Ben Macdui had a game of cards and
he won £20 off us.

Eck and Mike fae Dundee, 2 September 1998

IT NEVER RAINS BUT IT POURS

ALONG WITH LISTS of mountains climbed, the most popular topic that merits mention in the visitors' books is the weather... especially wet weather.

The gloomy hills around us frown
And we are none too merry,
For heavy rain is pouring down
And we've to go to Derry.

The path is rough but we are tough
And having dined full well,
With thoughtful heart we will depart
Although it rains like h---.

30 August 1928

Had very wet tramp to bothy, arrived there soaked to skin 3.10pm. Lit a blazing fire and dried some of our clothing. 5 o'clock, weather hellish. Did not stir out of doors after that except for water, owing to the terrible weather conditions prevailing on this part of God's earth.

Alfred W Raffan, 12 April 1931

A companion added: 'Tut! Tut!' after the word 'hellish'.

Great banks of fog are rolling down the sides of Ben Macdui and going tearing up Cairn Toul. Looks like a blanket being shaken.

M Mitchell, 1 June 1931

Corrour Bothy once again. The same old wind, and *still* more rain.

R Byers, 9 August 1931

Oh Cairngorms! I love your weather,
Away you rolling river.
It seems it's mist and rain forever.
Away I'm bound to go,
Across the wet Glen Lui.

                                                                    2 October 1931

It has rained intermittently all day and a high wind makes life a chilly
business. Several tons of bogwood were laboriously mined. We hope
some later arrivals will find it more flammable than we did. If bad
weather persists we will return to Linn of Dee tomorrow, though there
is likely to be trouble in crossing the Dee.

                                                                18 September 1935

Very impressed by the mountain scenery, which is similar to N. Wales
but much more remote & desolate. Weather cloudy, rotten for
London but the stuff the Scots call 'not bad'.

                                                   Geoff Peacock, London, 7 July 1938

The weather has been of a traditional Scottish nature: rain, sun, wind
and mist. We are homeward bound before the snow comes now!!

                                                             Andrew Stuart, 21 July 1938

Arrived last night in a sorry mess after falling into the rain-swollen
Dee. We were considerably cheered however by a cup of tea
provided by a kind stranger.

To write this we summoned the Muses,
Who refused without any excuses,
To set down this rhyme,
Would take too much time,
In this wettest of wet Lairig Gruses.

                                                                      10 July 1939

As we were nearing the summit [of Ben Macdui] the mist came down,
shutting out what might have been a wonderful view. By the time we
had reached the foot again the mist had gone and the sun was shining.
We were more than disappointed at the dirty trick the weather clerk
had played on us.

                                                         MM Gordon, 21 August 1939

Readers of those days would have known the 'weather clerk' to be an imaginary being who directed the weather.

We think we may have climbed Ben Macdui but, owing to the atmospheric conditions, hell knows where we've been.

DW Sayer, 1 September 1939

The raindrops came down like a wolf on the fold;
The bothy got flooded – its occupants cold:
Till they floated around on a heathery sea,
As the storm clouds rolled over the waters of Dee.

Bill Rynie, 8 July 1948

Met report: 17/10 cloud. Visibility: 0. Epicentre of earthquake half a mile up the glen. Avalanches and landslides intermittent. Water vapour content of air: 93%. Wind velocity: 104mph, with gusts rising to 148mph. 3cwt boulders blowing down the glen make walking difficult.

6 August 1951

No glint of sun up in the sky
A welcome to the climber's eye
Nought but heavy mist and rain
Oh why do I come back again?

Signed: The Bothy Poet, 20 May 1953

Coronation Day. Arrived at bothy yesterday after camping in the Lairig Ghru. Driving sleet and wind at gale force.

Miss Jessie Pack, 2 June 1953

Arrived 12 noon en route Coylumbridge to Derry Lodge. Torrential rain 12.30. Thankful to arrive dry and await passing shower. One member flaked out on bothy floor. 2nd member up to knees in marsh. 3rd member sufficiently alive to scribble.

John, 26 June 1954

A very welcome stop after swimming all the way from Braemar!

FB Gardner, 19 August 1955

[While walking through the Lairig Ghru] Sheets of rain came sweeping and driving over the tops. Ten minutes was enough to soak us thoroughly, and the account of the next hour and a half might perhaps be left unwritten. Let us suffice to say that we managed to dry off our feet considerably by wading the Dee in front of the bothy.

WD McTaggart and party, HMS *Ganges*, 2 July 1958

Arrived here 1 o'clock from Sinclair Memorial Hut. Weather bloody awful – drizzle and mist. We are soaked to the skin and are running around in shorts trying to keep warm.

Douglas Fowlie and Douglas Marr, 11 August 1966

It's been raining hard all night and it's noon now and the rains and wind drive on. Rain's coming down the chimney; it's impossible to get a fire going. Luckily I've got a gas burner and plenty of food, so I'm quite comfortable here waiting for these endless rains to leave. I really prefer this to civilisation.

Andy Mundell, 27 May 1972

Arrived in a downpour yesterday from Derry Lodge via White Bridge. Unfortunately we forgot to include umbrellas in our equipment, but our flippers and wet suits helped a great deal – made friends with lots of frogs on the way.

Morag McCallum & Elaine Shaw, 25 July 1972

But it doesn't always rain…

April 18 Arrived from Braemar. Heavy going through snow.

April 19 Devil's Point, Monadh Mor, Beinn Bhrotain. Wonderful weather. Sunbathed stripped in the snow at 3,200ft.

April 20 Another glorious day. Sunbathed in morning then climbed Carn a' Mhaim.

April 21 Yet another glorious day. G. Little climbed Cairn Toul while R. Little was afraid to venture out because of blistered face.

April 22 Phenomenal weather. Setting off 9.15 for Braemar and home in bright sunshine. Snow melting rapidly.

R Little and G Rennie, 22 April 1951

The next visitors arrived as the pair left.

Rennie and Little left here looking like a couple of boiled tomatoes.

22 April 1951

DON'T FORGET TO PACK YOUR THERMALS

MANY VISITORS TO Corrour seem unprepared for its lack of central heating.

> Coldest temperature ever recorded in the British Isles, minus 26 degrees Fahrenheit – 58 degrees of frost (minus 32 degrees Celsius) – was at the Corrour Bothy in the Cairngorms, some 2,000ft above sea-level. It was recorded on December 27, 1927, in a diary found near the bodies of two Glasgow geologists who died on the spot, victims of the cold [see Page 51].
>
> Montague Smith, 'Cold Fact', *Daily Mail*,
> 14 February 1947

The coldest official British temperature is -17°F (-22°C), recorded at Braemar in 1895 and 1982 and at Altnaharra in Sutherland in 1995.

> Spent one of the coldest nights alive… If this is summer, Lord help winter travellers.
>
> W Dickie, 9 August 1931

> Arrived from the ruined cottage of Allt-druie where we spent Friday night. Had rough going with very soft snow over the Lairig Ghru Saturday, taking about 10½ hours. Spent Sunday gathering roots and heather. Much colder than yesterday. Dee frozen over. Marvellous day with cloudless sky.
>
> 28 December 1935

> 4 orphans of the storm arrived from Aviemore after surviving 3 icy blizzards in the Lairig. Boots now walking themselves.
>
> R Stevenson, 17 May 1938

LAST WILL AND TESTAMENT OF A. & J. MUIR
On looking out of the bothy this morning we find it has been a
blizzard all night. There are very deep drifts of snow on every side.
Methinks we'd better gather more wood and hibernate.

A Muir, 2 January 1939

First it rained and then it blew,
Then it friz and then it snew,
Once more it rained and then it blew,
And then it friz and snew again.

James S Bufford, 22 October 1949

Storm has subsided. Calm and frosty. Setting off on ski over tops
to Speyside.

A Watson, 4 April 1950

Adam Watson (1930–2019) was 19 at the time. Inspired by
Seton Gordon, he went on to become the pre-eminent authority on
the Cairngorms and, among other achievements, wrote the comprehensive 1975 SMC guidebook to the range.

Another visitor arrived on the same day:

Walked up Lairig Ghru from Loch Morlich in hope of skiing on tops,
but weather closed down at noon. Arrived very wet – life saved by
Adam Watson's fire.

4 April 1950

This is an intriguing entry. Had Adam not yet left the bothy
when this next visitor arrived? Surely he hadn't left the fire still
blazing?

In 1955, several Rucksack Club parties assembled at the bothy
for an Easter meet.

The entire party creaked into action and craned their necks
towards the summit of Cairn Toul – a tiny point of snow pierc-
ing the deep blue sky infinitely far above them. It was a bright
cold morning with only a light north wind. The party moved
slowly – at first up easy slopes and then up steeper harder
snow. Experience and sure-footedness began to tell on the latter slopes and the party tended to split up... The wind had

dropped calm, all around us were sparkling sunlit peaks, and in general life was very good indeed.

Gordon and Keith stretched on ahead to the summit, where they were able to discard much clothing and stretch out in the brilliant wilderness of snow to let the heavenly sunshine penetrate their bodies... Ages later the rest of the party arrived and began their rest. Several snaps were taken.

Gordon and Keith were keen to go on and climb Braeriach, which they did, leaving the rest of the party to justify their existence by climbing another Munro on the way down – Devil's Point. G and K made good progress round the huge 4,000ft Garbh Choire. The weather remained perfect and the snow sparkled like a million diamonds. The snow was soft at times but it wasn't long before the summit of Braeriach was reached. The view was almost limitless. Cairn Toul and Angel's Peak were especially beautiful with the evening sun glinting across their high remote corries and ridges.

They made a quick sliding descent and made good time to the bothy. It was with great disgust that they found that the Devil's Point party had not yet returned. Further investigation revealed its members in various stages and methods of descent from the Devil's Point col. All bodies having been accounted for, a long-lasting and very welcome meal was enjoyed by all.

Rucksack Club Easter meet, March 1955

A few inches of snow during the night, and still blowing like fury from the north; these are conditions one looks for in January. Sat in and read a book all yesterday – no fun in going out in this. Saw a large flock of brass monkeys fleeing to the south.

N Phillip, Ealing Cycling Club (but walking this time),
17 October 1955

In 1955–6, Patrick Baird, Arctic explorer and Aberdeen University Research Fellow, set up a weather station on Ben Macdui and spent a year studying the snow beds in the 'Snowy Corrie' (Garbh Uisge Mor), just north-east of the summit. Here, he claimed, 'one can glissade any month of the year'. In total he made 36 visits, including from Corrour.

Between the end of April (maximum) and the end of September 1956, the surface went down by 27 feet – but there was still a foot or two left.

PD Baird, 'Weather and Snow on Ben Macdhui', CCJ No 91, 1957

Baird wasn't the first to be fascinated by the semi-permanent snowbeds of the Cairngorms. The most persistent lie at the head of Garbh Choire Mor – the sheltered inner corrie at the head of Garbh Choire. Large volumes of snow accumulate here at the foot of the headwall crags after being blown off the windswept plateau above. In summer the snow thaws into a row of three distinct patches, known as Michaelmas Fare, Sphinx and Pinnacles. One of the earliest visitors to be captivated by them was Caleb Cash who, after he first saw them from the plateau rim in 1894, was drawn back to view them again and again.

From then until 1959, all three patches disappeared only twice – in 1933 and 1947. They have disappeared a few more times since and in 2017 and 2018 disappeared in consecutive years for the first time since records began in the 19th century. In his writing, Cash makes no reference to Corrour Bothy but he must have been familiar with it, even if it is unclear whether he ever approached Garbh Coire from the Lairig Ghru.

In the 1960s, the Rucksack Club and Geography Department of Dundee University (then Queen's College, University of St Andrews) conducted a scientific survey of the snowbeds. With heavy surveying equipment, the easiest approach route was from Linn of Dee and parties often visited or stayed at Corrour en route. When the survey began in October 1965, the winter snow had already begun to accumulate.

The snow-bed consisted of two lobes, one slightly larger than the other. The smaller lobe was about 100ft across and 150ft long and at the 'schrund' some 20ft deep.

WG Berry, 'Salute to Garbh Coire', SMCJ No 158, 1967

Heavy snow prevented further work until March 1966, although several attempts were made to reach the corrie during the winter. A November attempt was led by Tony Bellhouse (club president) and Brian Dodson (vice-president). I have Tony to thank for leading me over Aonach Eagach on my first ever day on a Scottish mountain, which instilled a lifelong passion. He and Brian had the admirable trait of being unflappable on the hill and they were never averse to a spot of banter to lighten the mood.

Rucksack Club party, on the way to continue work in Garbh Choire Mor, arrived 1pm in worsening weather. Snow was drifting and wind too violent to allow us to venture on to the corrie that day. Spent a comfortable night and awoke at 4am to go up to the corrie. Weather was impossible, however, so we continued to spend a comfortable night! Breakfast at 8.30. Left at 11.00am for Derry. Thank goodness for Corrour. We will return and try again!! (Ha! Ha!)

Tony Bellhouse, 27 November 1965

How do you know weather impassable at 4am? Might have guessed you'd stoop to lying to get an extra few hours kip!

Brian Dodson, 27 November 1965

Other visitors' book entries also testify to the severity of that winter.

Spent one of the coldest nights in history doing physical jerks in an attempt to get defrosted. Awoke to find boots solid and socks like cast iron, but with stove going full blast we soon toasted them back to life... Attempted to climb first gully in Glen Geusachan on Devil's Point but were stopped by a somewhat precipitous cornice.

Jim Cruikshank, 27 December 965

In February 1966, another Rucksack Club survey party also failed to make much progress past Corrour:

[Saturday] Arrived from Derry at 11.45am on ski. Continuing up to Garbh Choire Mhor to camp for the night. No snow holes for us. Return tomorrow. [Added later] Returned at 3pm. High wind and poor visibility – no use for survey.

[Sunday] Spent night here but was same on Sunday. Left at 11.30am for Derry.

R Thompson with two others, 18–19 February 1966

Ritchie was by far the best climber in the club at the time. I was in awe of his ability. He seemed to defy gravity. He taught me how to crampon on Glen Coe's Buachaille Etive Mor.

A month later, the corrie was full of avalanche debris. By April, the survey equipment left in place had been buried or destroyed. By May, snow had cleared the lower corrie.

Arrived in cruel weather from White Bridge. We intend to stay for a few days on a survey.

Staff Nurse S Lenton & Student Nurse D Harle,
Tower Hospital Male Nurses Expedition,
Leicester, 2 May 1966

The nature of this survey is unknown, but the Rucksack Club was in Garbh Coire again soon afterwards.

Arrived here 12pm on 6th in sleet after taking an hour to find the bothy – easier to find the bogs – completed survey, returning to Derry 6pm on 7th.

Lew Reay, Rucksack Club, 7 May 1966

In June, a party camped in the corrie for two weeks and at last made significant progress. They studied not only the still extensive upper-corrie snow-bed but also the ecological habitat (mosses, insects, small mammals etc) and the rate of landscape erosion caused by the periglacial conditions. By July, the upper corrie snow-bed had divided into two parts, of which the upper was still 250ft long. By August, it was 150ft long and, by September, only 45ft long. This was less than the previous year but was probably affected by survey activity, which required digging holes in it. In October, the snow began to fall again. It had been an eventful year.

3 very cold nights. Thank goodness I had my electric blanket with me.

Ronnie Black, 9 January 1970

The Trans-Arctic Expedition of Richards, Jenkins and Culmore took a wrong turning at the North Pole and ended up here. Very nice place here if you like freezing your b-------s off.

23 June 1971.

Lambkins gambolling full of frolics,
Frozen solid are their bollix,
Climbers clinging to the rocks,
Frozen solid are their hands.

8 May 1972

Came tumbling down from Cairn Toul to avoid what anywhere
else would be called a blizzard but is probably regarded here as a
moderately high wind with lumps of ice in it.

Jim Craigon, 9 May 1972

'Twas in Corrour at Christmas
Or else at Hogmanay,
And it was bloody freezing
That's all that we can say.

Syd Scroggie, Bothy Graffiti, in *Give Me The Hills*, 1978

Struggled from Bynack, mostly up to knees in snow. Refreshing wade
through Geldie Burn! Reached Corrour at 4pm as darkness fell.
Corrour life-saving. Blizzard.

20 December 1982

Arrived Blair Atholl. Went up Glen Tilt. Good skiing to Falls of Tarf –
camped there overnight. Following day walked most of way to Bynack
Lodge – nice lawn so decided to camp. Drizzly morning. Decided to
frequent Corrour Bothy... Snow just soft and wet enough to slow you
down and wet your feet and not enough to ski on. Got back on skis
about 4 miles from bothy. Skied to river, saw bridge and crossed – but
it isn't long enough (ie river bigger than bridge). Managed to jump,
however. Could not see path in snow drifts. White stuff gave way and
disappeared down hole, me with it. Damn cold, this water. Rucksack
thankfully stopped rest of me going down. Pulled myself out (not
easy when your feet aren't on the bottom) and blow me if I didn't go
down another one – must be enjoying this, he's done it twice already.
Needless to say, arrived at bothy cold and wet. Wish I had a fire. Wind
is howling, sky is clearing, temperature is dropping. To think I could
have been home in front of the fire having opened Christmas presents,

stuffed turkey down me and had a double helping of Christmas pud
and I gave it all up for this.

25 December 1982

Arrived from Braemar yesterday and camped by the river. No chance
of reaching Aviemore in these conditions, so we're heading to Blair
Atholl by Glen Tilt with the gale behind us (hopefully).

Ralph and Judith, 2 April 1983

An embarrassingly misleading entry by myself. Instead of heading for Blair Atholl, a brief clearing in the weather lured us up the
Lairig, only to be roundly rebuffed by blizzard conditions near the
summit. We retreated to our riverside camp spot again, where our
tent was ripped to shreds by the wind and we had to seek refuge in
the crowded bothy. It may well have saved our lives. Others arrived
the following morning in a bad state, having spent the night in a
snow hole.

For many of us who love the Cairngorms, they are nevertheless
at their most alluring in winter. After our night in the bothy, the
weather cleared and we made it over the summit of the Lairig to
Aviemore in sparkling snow conditions.

We have just walked up from Aviemore through the Lairig Ghru on
a glorious day. After threatening all day to go for a dip, Ben finally
decided that if he didn't go in the Pools of Dee he would never get a
swim in. All we could do was watch in horror as he lowered himself
into what must be the equivalent of liquid nitrogen, so if anything
snaps off he knows who to blame.

9 July 1983

It's cold, wet and windy, but it's Bonnie Scotland and I love it. I'll be
back in October when it's even colder.

Laurence Davey, 16 years old, Surrey, 2 August 1996

It was a cold but clear and crisp afternoon as I approached the
summit of Macdui, when out of the wild blue yonder came angry
swirling clouds bearing the first snow of the season. If this is the kind
of weather you get under Scottish rule you can stick devolution.
Even the Grey Man was loath to put in an appearance. I headed
straight down here for sanctuary. Never was a bothy more welcome.

Young Fella, 12 September 1997

I will not bore you with complaints of being cold, wet and sore. But as we sit here and dream of food and warmth, we would only dream of snow and ice if we did have food and warmth. So instead of talking rain and midges, let's talk of snow and ice and all things NICE!

Derek, 16 February 1998

Great to see the ptarmigan changing to their winter plumage already. Can't wait for the snow so we can come back on the skis. Roll on winter!

Simon Hamm, Outward Bound Scotland, 26 September 1998

A whopping 7 hour trudge through thigh-deep drifts from Bob Scott's. Relieved to get here and grateful for the shelter. Went on to Garbh Coire and Falls of Dee. Beautiful ice shapes in and over the river.

Rob P, 2 February 2019

ADVENTUROUS ESCAPADES

MANY WHO VISIT Corrour find the experience more adventurous than anticipated.

My next winter expedition had both its comic and almost tragic side... The drive from Ballater to Braemar was made on wheels; from Braemar to Derry Lodge it was done in sleighs.

[Snow conditions thwarted an attempt on Derry Cairngorm]

In these circumstances we returned to Braemar, after making an unpleasant slip on the frozen slope, the consequence of which was rather unpleasant for the one of us who wore the kilt.

Alex Inkson McConnochie, 'The Cairngorms in Winter',
SMCJ Vol 1, 1891

On our way we passed the Luibeg Cottage. Not a living soul was to be seen or heard; only our footsteps broke the silence of the night. We endeavoured to keep to the path, but more than once measured our full length on the heather... Everything around us was dark and eerie, and the rain came down in torrents before we reached the Dee.

Henry C Dugan, 'A Midnight Experience at the Derry',
CCJ NO 71, 1926

Two members spent a fortnight at Corrour Bothy, during which they climbed Ben MacDui three times, Cairntoul twice, and Cairngorm and Derry Cairngorm, Carn a' Mhaim, Beinn Bhrotain and Monadh Mor once. At the end of a week they visited Braemar to obtain fresh supplies.

They climbed Cairngorm by crossing over Ben Macdui. On the return journey they made the descent to the Shelter Stone and Loch Avon. They then climbed up a chimney behind the Shelter Stone

(Pinnacle Gully) and only just managed to reach the top by lying flat against a waterfall. As it had been raining previously, however, their clothes were already saturated with water.

Having arrived at the top, they decided that, with the mist hiding everything, the only sure way was to keep on climbing until they reached the cairn of Ben Macdui again. This they did after an eerie tramp over the vast plateau of Ben Macdui in thick mist and soaking clothes. Having arrived at the cairn, the last stage back to the bothy was completed in less than three quarters of an hour thanks to a long snow drift in the Tailors' Corrie, down which they skated or rolled with no equilibrium permitted!

AA Blyth-Martin and P Ritchie,
Rucksack Club meet, June 1927

Since we were here last – on 5th August – we have covered abut 300 miles on foot. We have had gorgeous weather nearly all the time… Of the different types of hills we have seen we like the Cairngorms best.

Only the road and the dawn,
The sun, the wind and the rain,
The watch-fire under the stars,
And sleep and the road again.

Lorna G Hay (Aberdeen Girls' High School), with three
other girls, 28 August 1931

This is the only verified teenage entry, and one of the few existing female records, in the pre-war visitors' books. The four intrepid girls had been out for four weeks and even climbed a few Cuillin.

Two well-known mountaineers, Messrs George Shand and WD Hutcheon, Turriff, claim to have broken the six-peak record, with a time of under thirteen and a half hours… Setting out from their car at Loch Builg at 8.45pm on Saturday night, the Turriff men were on the 'tops' at the following times – Beinn a' Bhuird 10.50pm, Ben Avon 12am, Cairngorm 3.45am, Ben Macdhui 5.20am, Braeriach 7.15am, Cairntoul 9.30am, and down at Corrour Bothy at 10.10am.

Aberdeen Journal, 27 June 1933

Fine cloud effects were seen as I went up Coire Odhar to Devil's
Point. A small rainbow appeared to lie on the Lairig path. The bow
expanded as I climbed, until it topped the Macdui ridge.

John Bell, 11 July 1936

New Year 1937 was a busy time in the Cairngorms.

Dundee members of Creag Dhu Climbing Club are to spend New
Year's Day at Corrour Bothy in the Cairngorms. The winter meet
of the club is being held there and will be attended by a Dundee
party of six and a Glasgow party of 15.

...

Over 40 members of the Cairngorm Club arrived at the Inver-
cauld Arms Hotel, Braemar, yesterday for their New Year's Day
meet. No climbing was done yesterday, but Lochnagar will be
attacked today.

...

Several Dundee members of the Grampian Club brought in the
New Year in Glen Clova. They arrived at the Ogilvy Arms Hotel,
Milton of Glen Clova, last night in heavy rain. Today they intend
to do some climbing on the surrounding hills.

'New Year Greetings on Cairngorms', *Dundee Courier*,
1 January 1937

It didn't all go according to plan, as the Courier reported the
following day.

Blizzards on Ben MacDhui defeated attempts to conquer the
mountain, but Lochnagar was climbed by two parties. Six made
the attempt on Ben Macdhui. Nineteen attempted the ascent of
Lochnagar from the north-west, but only five reached the summit,
the remainder having given up the struggle against the blizzard.

'Climbers Brave Rain and Snow', *Dundee Courier*,
2 January 1937

The visitors' book confirms that the bad weather continued for
some time.

Eleven hardy mountaineers well equipped with axes, maps and
compasses set off confidently to make Einich bothy. Unfortunately

one compass passed in its checks and the other didn't agree with the party, so after traipsing around in an unsympathetic snowstorm the party decided to take the first available route down... A cold, short argument with a cornice forced a descent into a mysterious corrie. When the party's brains had thawed sufficiently it was decided that we had landed at Lochan Uaine below Cairn Toul. The party covered their ignominious retreat by saying that Corrour was as good a bothy as Einich any day. So here we are back again after a full day's parade over the ridges, still alive and happy. Pass that drum of tea, please.

D Browning, 4 January 1937

Best walk I have had on this earth led by a bothy-mate. Cairn Toul and Braeraith [sic] amid clouds broken at intervals and so revealing views so beautiful that today will never be forgotten.

[The following day] Bathed in the 1st Pool of Dee at 8.30am, climbed March Burn to Ben Macdhui.

[The following day] Goodbye to Corrour Bothy with real regrets.

Geoff Peacock, 21 July 1938

[After crossing to Loch Avon via the Cairn Gorm plateau] We returned via Loch Etchachan to Ben Macdhui, which was covered with mist blown in our faces with terrific force by the gale. We were forced to lie down in places, it being impossible to keep upright in the face of the gusts. Had difficulty locating the Tailors Burn, but a rift in the mist showed us our route and we braved our way downwards still facing the hurricane. We were both suffering from fatigue-shock and were never more delighted than on seeing this Highland Home.

Dead good going! Two magnificent days in the Cairngorms and a memory which we'll never forget.

JR Dyett, 8 June 1939

LONE SASSENACH DEFIES CAIRNGORMS
[After walking from Aviemore and climbing over Cairn Gorm to descend to the Shelter Stone at Loch Avon] Scrambling down here I strained a muscle in my left knee, nothing serious, but it made

putting this leg to the ground very painful. Limped along to where
the Shelter Stone should be but, not having read about where to find
it before and everything, being obliterated by mist I couldn't find it.
It being out of the question to go back, the only alternative was to
climb out again and down to the Lairig and make for the bothy.

Looking up the cataract of the Feith Buidhe to the great tracts of
mist and snow was rather frightening, but I started off up the sloping
and slippery rocks, dragging the injured leg after me. I could not see
where the cataract was coming from and had to be careful not to
start the snow moving. It seemed like climbing into the very heart
of nature.

Eventually I reached the top, staggered along to Lochan Buidhe and
down the March Burn. The wind took the cap over my head and flung
me down a long way, injuring my wrist, which began to drip blood
steadily, and tearing the sleeve of my jacket. Drenched and weary,
I arrived at the familiar Lairig and made off down the path for the
bothy. Walked through the river as I was, for I could get no wetter.

R Bridges, 25 June 1939

The walk through Rothiemurchus Forest was lovely, the sun shining. As
we ascended up through the pass the rain came down and it was jolly
cold… We met two people who doctored up Joyce's blister. Then we
met a cyclist with his bike on his back. We waded through the Dee and
here we are now in Corrour Bothy, seated before a blazing fire with
our shoes and stockings up to dry.

Nancy Keay, with Sheila Murdoch and Joyce Campbell,
1 August 1939

Walked up the Lairig as far as Garbh Coire and climbed into Core
Bhrochain. This is a grand corrie. Great fun here for the boulder
hopper, the rock scrambler, and even some juicy bits for those guys
and gals who hang by their fingers and eyebrows to thousand-foot
vertical rock faces.

W Smith, 17 August 1939

We arrived here today after spending the night on the summit of
Ben Macdhui… We dug a hole for our tent in the ruins of the old
Ordnance Survey hut. Finally snuggled down about 10pm and slept

the old year out. Awoke about 1am and peeped out to a night of stars and moonlight.

The moon was encircled by a perfect lunar rainbow and the still, white silence was arctic in its intensity. The cold, however, shortened our stargazing considerably and drove us back to the comparative warmth of our bags, where we slept on and off till the first rays of the sun struck the summit and enticed us from the warmth of our bags – after breakfast – out to a glorious dawn.

The whole world seemed to be a dazzling spectacle of glistening white, and the sight of good old King Sol sent us cheering up to the cairn, there to dance up and down like two arctic madmen...

We then made for Corrour, which we reached without incident. However, as the bothy was half-full of several notorious members of the Creag Dhubh, we have no doubt that incidents will develop.

David Browning (CAF Glasgow), 1 January 1940

The stone ruins of the os hut, aka the Sappers' Bothy, lie just southeast of the summit at NN 991988. The hut was built around 1847 to house surveyors during the Principal Triangulation of Britain.

Browning's entry prompted a rival reply from the Creag Dhu club.

Arrived here on Sunday 31st. Weather was perfect but has now broken down today. Thanks to our usual vigilance we managed to leave with the gear we arrived with, a surprising fact given the presence in the bothy of several notorious West of Scotland mountaineers. I now close and wish the many mountaineers who come here a prosperous and happy new year.

Charles Robertson (Creag Dhu), 3 January 1940

Arrived at Corrour Bothy today at 2.30. My first hike. It may not seem much to many a hiker. But I am glad I have come this far.

Sheila Raitt, 10 years old, 21 August 1948

Perfect day for climbing. Went over shoulder of Ben Macdhui to Cairn Gorm. On way back braved storm (of abuse) to swim in Pools of Dee while others contented with a paddle... Evening meal (seven course) lasted for three hours. Winds rose both inside and outside the bothy.

William Bain, 15 September 1950

Left Glenmore Lodge (Rothiemurchus) via Creag an Leth-choin and
Ben Macdhui. Weather very good, and we had sunshine most of the
time. From the top of Creag an Leth-choin we had a marvellous view.
There were huge cracks in the snow where tons had broken away
from Tailors' Corrie.

Dick Gowers, 9 July 1951

August 2. Arrived 10.30pm from other side of the River Tilt, where
I camped the previous night, camping rucksack weighing 50lbs (felt
like 500lbs). Too dark to find stepping stones so I waded across burn
& got boots full of water. How glorious to be greeted with a glowing
fire & hot cup of tea.

August 3 [After walking over Cairn Toul to Braeriach] Arrived
back pretty exhausted at 10.45pm – too tired to eat. Found 6 already
bedded down – again I was the only female.

August 4. Up Ben Macdhui via Tailor's Burn. Met 2 wild Scotsmen
at summit who, seeing me through the mist, mistook me for the Grey
Man. [She continued down to the Shelter Stone] Found 1 chap only,
busy roasting a ptarmigan he had killed with a stick... Up the Ben
again via Loch Etchachan and back down to bothy via Tailors' Burn.
Found bothy fully occupied by a dozen people. 3 other girls to keep
me company.

Joan M Winfield, 2–4 August 1951

Climbed up into Garbh Coire Dhaidh and scrambled up to the
plateau along the side of the falling Dee. Found a charming little pool
into which the water was falling (about a third of the way up the cliff).
We dallied there, and each partook of a shower – most refreshing.
Continued to follow the stream to the Wells of Dee and on to
Angel's Peak. Here we witnessed my first Brocken Spectre. Back to
the bothy via Cairn Toul.

14 September 1952

Last Wednesday the RAF thought we were worth a few days leave and
so, taking a free warrant, we travelled up from our camp (good old
Yatesbury) near Swindon, Wilts., and arrived at Kincraig Station at
7.40am Friday. This was our first mistake as we meant to get out at
Aviemore. After a tar lorry had given us a lift to Aviemore, we did a

little shopping and took a walk to Loch an Eilean. We spent Friday night at Aviemore YH.

On Saturday we set out for Braeriach and Cairn Toul via Glen Einich and the Beanaidh path. We arrived here at about 9 o'clock, cooked a meal and went straight to bed. The weather was not too bad, cloudy but not cold, but when we woke up this morning the sky was clearer and the sun shining.

Well, in a few minutes we will be off for Braemar. We hope to return to Aviemore via the Shelter Stone. And don't forget our motto: THERE'S A PLACE FOR YOU IN THE R.A.F. and watch it.

Jack. JD Lewis, 18 June 1955

The Yatesbury camp closed in 1965.

We travelled far, we travelled wide,
Could not keep no pace nor stride,
But through the Lairig Ghru we went,
There was no place to pitch a tent.
Ben Mac Dui, he stood there,
For us he did not care.
All the road our feet were sore,
But we will reach our destination:
(Aviemore)

Rocky Mulligan, 25 August 1955

On the Ben's summit we couldn't see a sausage. Although there was plenty of orange peel up there. The top was a fog, in which we succeeded in getting lost, nearly descending to the lochs instead of the pass. With profound thanks we re-reached the summit and began again, going due south from the top until the steep edge of the pass was reached then following the contours round to the Taillear Burn.

Donald Knight and Derek Knight, 22 August 1958

The Edinburgh Company of Boys Brigade
Duke of Edinburgh Award Gold Standard Expedition

When these boys finish this course they will be the first [Duke of Edinburgh] Golden award in Edinburgh. There was another party of younger boys who found that the experience gained on

this trip would be invaluable when they reach the age for entering
the competition.

Staff Sgt T Dundas Esq, 14 September 1958

Came up on Friday night. Miss Bauman is stimulating company.
Saturday afternoon went via Cairn Toul and Braeriach. Caught
in thunderstorm on Angel's Peak and finished circuit in rain
and heavy mist – interesting. Today (Sunday) heading out,
but will look up Sputan Dearg to see if there are any tigers
hanging about.

David Bain, 19 June 1966

One trusts a sighting of the 'tigers' (presumably rock climbers)
was as stimulating as his night in the bothy with Miss Bauman.

Arrived here Thursday and spent night singing and jigging. Comments
from all that they had seen nothing like it before at Corrour. Went up
Garbh Coire Mor on Friday & built snow hole (deluxe model). Spent
comfortable night in it and only left it regrettably at noon. Climbed
Cairn Toul on way back to Derry Lodge.

Barbara Buchan, 6 January 1966

Royal Marine Reserve. From Cairn Gorm – Ben Macdhui –
misty. Stayed night. Return to Aviemore by Cairn Toul/Braeriach.

Alan Blackshaw (& companions), 28 March 1970

Royal Marine Reserve Commando party. Same two-day route
in reverse.

Alan Blackshaw, Mike Lowe, 1 August 1970

Alan Blackshaw (1933–2011) was a mountaineer, skier and lover
of the Cairngorms who became President of a number of mountaineering bodies, including the British Mountaineering Council, the Ski
Club of Great Britain and the Alpine Club. From 1956 to 1974 he
was a mountain warfare instructor in the Royal Marine Reserve,
during which time he wrote the seminal 1965 manual 'Mountaineering: From Hill Walking to Alpine Climbing'. Known simply as
'Blackshaw', it was the go-to fount of all wisdom for budding hill-
men of the time such as myself.

Mountaineering may come to mean much more than a sport; you may find it a philosophy of living. If you do, and I hope you may, then you and the mountains will be inseparable through life.

Alan Blackshaw, 'Mountaineering:
From Hill Walking to Alpine Climbing', 1965

Left Crewe at midnight by sleeper – arrived Aviemore 8am. Straight up to Cairn Gorm chairlift then marvellous but exhausting day across the plateau to Ben Macdui. Snow very deep of top, occasionally rather soft. Snow level about 3,300ft. Weather dry, calm and clear, with spells of really hot sunshine – quite a change! Tomorrow plan to return to Aviemore via Cairn Toul and Braeriach. Then back by sleeper to Crewe, arriving 4.00am – no doubt in no fit state for work the following day!

Tony Watson, 14 May 1977

Lots of weather... En route to somewhere.

Bob, 26 May 1996

En route to the top of somewhere.
We came, we saw the inside of a cloud, we conquered something.

The North of Tyne Search and Rescue Team, 26 May 1996

Coming off Ben Macdui... I dropped through the cloud to find myself facing Devil's Point with Corrour plainly visible below it. What threw me completely for a minute was the sight of the river flowing uphill. So striking is the illusion that for a second I thought I was looking north and the river was flowing towards me. Has anyone else noticed this?

Terry Shaw, 9 June 1996

I am Cpl *illegible* of the Royal Military Police (T.A.) and I'm on a bit of a ramble through the Scottish countryside! Whilst the bad guys seem to have got away this time, I've decided to give up the chase and enjoy myself instead. To the Devil's Point. By the left...

4 August 1996

I'm supposed to be in Feshie doing PHD fieldwork but got itchy feet
and did Carn Ban Mor and other Feshie Munro + Braeriach/Cairn
Toul/Devil's Point etc. Today Carn a' Mhaim/Macdui/Beinn
Mheadhoin/Derry Cairngorm. Tomorrow back to Feshie via Monadh
Mor etc. By that time I'll be too knackered to do any fieldwork so I'll
tell my boss I got rained off. Hopefully if my boss ever gets to read this
I'll have got my PHD and all will be well. (Who am I kidding?) Nice bothy,
nice hills, nice company, noisy mice.

Simon Hinchcliffe, 7 August 1996

Did my first Munro today – Devil's Point. We went also to Cairn
Toul, but on our way clouds were coming and we decided to go back.
But still, the beginning is there. Only 200-something more! I like
it here.

9 September 1996

Thank God for the bothy. Having crawled the 4km from where I badly
hurt my ankle, it was such a joy to find a refuge. However, as a fellow
hillwalker, I would have appreciated some help from the people at the
bothy, rather than being stranded half-way up the slope while they
were warm and dry. Someday it may be YOU that wants rescuing.

Jennie, 16 July 1997

To leave a young lady half-way up a scree slope with a badly injured leg?
Shame on you. I stayed over to help and had to raid the emergency tin
to supplement rapidly diminishing food supplies. Thanks to the visitors
who have passed through since with offers of help and sandwiches etc.
Three cheers for the local ranger and mountain rescue boys for coming
as Jennie was still too badly injured to travel herself.

JC, 16 July 1997

I'd like to give a special mention to Carn a' Mhaim. Yes, that is the
mountain you're looking at out of the window (nice, ain't it?). This
gets a special mention and a prominent place in my memory as it was
my 100th Munro. Had an excellent week bagging 16 Munros. Off now
to Aviemore to celebrate.

Joseph 'The Geordie', exiled in Edinburgh, 14 August 1997

Would really recommend circuit of Glen Geusachan as a day's walk.
How could Ralph Storer not include it in his *100 Best Routes on
Scottish Mountains?*

Mick Kay, 14 August 1997

In my defence, I did not include it because the walks in that
book are circular routes from a roadside, not from a remote bothy.

Walked (or stumbled) from Loch Morlich yesterday. I suppose
I enjoyed it really. Never done anything like this before. Shame the
view was obscured by the mist. Could have been spectacular.

Kate Bonney, Gold Duke of Edinburgh Award, 7 June 1998

High Peaks Duathlon Challenge completed today. Challenge was: all
Welsh 3000s peaks, all English 3000s peaks, all Scottish 4000s peaks.
Cycling in-between. Total days to complete: 8. Well done, boys.

Stewart McKinnon, John McMillan & Kenny Murray,
18 July 1998

Our first time in the Cairngorms – awesome. Up against Mother
Nature she would win so easily, but thanks to Lowe Alpine and
Vango, and map and compass, we're still here. Remember Edward
Whymper: 'Do nothing in haste; look well to each step; and from the
beginning think what may be the end.' Think of this constantly and
you will survive.

Revo, 13 October 1998

Accompanied by his guide, Edward Whymper (1840–1911)
was the first person to reach the summit of the Matterhorn in
1865. The quote is from his classic book *Scrambles Amongst
the Alps*.

We lost our good friend R--- up on Devil's Point, but he was a bit of a
t--- so he won't be too missed. The rest of the DOE group are making
our way up the valley for a well-earned kip somewhere sheltered. If
R--- does show up, please send him the other way.

17 July 2016

CLIMBING CAPERS

CLIMBERS VISITED CORROUR and its watcher long before it became an open bothy, so when the last watcher left in 1920 it was natural for them to use it as a base for pioneering climbs in the great corries that flank the Lairig Ghru.

An intense frost held the air... After an early breakfast, cooked on our 'Optimus' stove, we felt much more comfortable. By this time the sun was rising, and from the bothy door we were witness of a beautiful scene... The two bluff shoulders of Ben Macdhui were clothed in a dazzling mantle of snow, while the snow in the corrie between, on which the first rays of the dawning sun were striking, was tinted a glorious crimson, giving the impression of a big crimson cloudbank... Soon the whole valley was ablaze with light... The sky was now an intense, clear blue, and the hills stood out in wonderful relief owing to the clarity and brightness of the atmosphere.

...

Crossing the snow-filled corrie [Coire Clach nan Taillear – the Tailors' Corrie] with difficulty, we followed the shoulder of Ben Macdhui, keeping to the exposed part from which the fierce blasts had blown the powdery snow, leaving the remainder in a hard beaten state, which gave ideal foothold... By a happy chance we came out near the cairn, which was a frozen mass of snow about twice its normal height, having a very grotesque sight in the swirling mist.

...

We amused ourselves by glissading down the steep slopes and found it a rapid mode of descent although somersaults were numerous.

'A Winter Climb on Ben Macdhui', *Dundee Courier*,
7 January 1926

In March 1931, two SMC members spent a week at Corrour. After
detraining at Blair Atholl they walked through Glen Tilt to lodging in Inverey before continuing to Derry Lodge. Here they picked
up 250lbs of provisions they'd had pre-delivered, including 1cwt of
coal. It required three trips to carry this load to Corrour, where they
were fortunate enough to find a snow bridge over the Dee. In fine
weather at the start of the week, they made the first ascent of the
Braeriach Pinnacle in Coire Bhrotain from below.

> We crossed the foot of the East Gully and continued our traverse
> leading to the Central Buttress Gully... The ridge from here to the
> top of the Braeriach Pinnacle was a delightful climb. Some of the
> rock needed careful testing, but there was no difficulty. The top of
> the pinnacle is a short level ridge, overlapping the east branch of
> the gully, with the final summit rising from its eastern end. Here,
> supported by sound rock on each side, are two strips of incred-
> ibly rotten stuff, which looks as if it might fall into the gully at
> any moment. This last and only obstacle, more sensational than
> difficult, was successfully overcome, and a minute later we stood
> on the highest point.
>
> PD Baird and RN Traquair, 'A Week at Corrour Bothy',
> SMCJ No 112, 1932

Later in the week the weather turned and, in an attempt to
climb the Black Pinnacle in Coire Bhrochain, they became disoriented and lost in a whiteout so complete it was 'impossible to see
the snow we stood on'. After that they needed a break.

> The next day was spent in idleness and luxury. We walked down
> to Braemar, enjoyed a shave, lunched at the hotel, and hired a car
> to take us home (to Inverey).
>
> PD Baird and RN Traquair, 'A Week at Corrour Bothy',
> SMCJ No 112, 1932

On their last day they 'ran hard uphill' on Beinn a' Ghlo, pro-
pelled by 'terrific' gusts of wind, after which they enjoyed a good
tea in Blair Atholl before boarding the train home.

We attempted some rock climbing but were always stopped by
pitches over which we novices could not get. Finally scrambled on top

via a grassy scree. Released a balloon from the summit in a hurricane. Crossed to Beinn Bhrotain, where we ambled from blaeberry bush to blaeberry bush, up a gully on the north face where we reached a 15-foot pitch near the top. When the rock started falling away at our hands and feet we gave up in disgust, and after reconciling ourselves with blaeberries (large ones), we returned.

E Rothney, 1 October 1931

Travelled in rubbers and were able to make better time than on our previous day's trip on Thursday last when, owing to rain, had our boots on (Braeriach to The Devil's Point, nailed boots). Very sunny on top and powerfully blowy.

Walter Gray, 26 July 1937

For those who could afford them, mountain boots of the time used a variety of specialised nails to improve traction on soles. Others simply climbed in workers' hobnailed boots. Vibram, invented in Italy in 1937, did not become routinely available in the UK until the 1950s. 'Rubbers' were any soft-soled boots or shoes. Rock climbers might wear plimsolls, tennis shoes or even rope-soled shoes.

Climbed to top of Coire an Toul and glissaded into Glen Dee and returned to bothy on account of bad weather.

J Nimlin, 5 January 1938

Devil's Point. Honourable failure through discretion and soft snow. Nix tam alta erat.

GM Smith, 28 April 1940

Nix tam alta erat: The snow was so deep.

Newcomers will have noticed the tremendous fall of rock off the face of the Devil's Point. Lots more to come yet if one studies the angle at which some of the rock rests on the slabs. How are the mighty fallen.

R Reid, 23 May 1940

Inspected snowfield in the Garbh Coire. Tried to cross it and made an involuntary glissade.

John M McCabe, 24 June 1943

Climbed Devil's Point by small gully on the North East face. The
route was firstly up slab which was coated with water and slime
and the rest of the climb consisted of rock and vegetation, with a
100ft snow pitch at the summit. Climbed Cairn Toul by walking to
the summit by Coire Odhar and the Soldiers' Corrie. Glissaded into
Coire ant-Sabhail and descended by the ridge to the bothy. As we
were approaching bothy the weather broke and it began to snow
heavily. The time is now 10.35 and we are leaving Corrour for Luibeg.
It is, incidentally, still snowing.

David Brown, 6 April 1949

Left 10am for Coire Bhrochain. Ice falling continually from rocks.
Climbed Pyramus Gully by rib in its centre – very enjoyable. Thick
mist on top (*of Braeriach*). Down by long glissade in Garbh Coire
Dhaidh. Back at 8.00pm.

William Brooker, 12 April 1950

Bill Brooker (1931–2011) was one of the post-war generation of
north-east climbers who pioneered challenging rock and ice routes
in the 1950s. Among other achievements, he made the first winter
ascents of Eagle Ridge on Lochnagar (with Tom Patey and Mike
Taylor) and Mitre Ridge on Beinn a' Bhuird (with Tom Patey). He
later became president of the Scottish Mountaineering Club.

Rescued two climbers from chock stone gully [sic]. Never been so
glad to see the bothy in all my born days. Reached here after
travelling 4hrs in dark and mud.

Alastair Watson, 17 April 1950

Chokestone Gully, named for the huge chockstone on its final
pitch, is a prominent gully on Sgor an Lochain Uaine on the south
side of Garbh Coire. It was first climbed in summer in 1911 and is
the most popular climb mentioned in the visitors' books.

A quick foray was made into Garbh Coire… and two gullies were
climbed… The leftmost had a promising start but soon degenerated
into a scree shoot between high walls. However, it redeemed itself by
providing a difficult little chimney (cold water laid on) just before the exit.

The other one, whose upper half could not be seen in the mist, looked good at its commencement. Scree patches alternating with small mossy pitches gave good scrambling, and at the neck the left containing wall gave us much food for thought. Huge pillars of granite leaning drunkenly over the gully, with seemingly no visible means of support, made us skip up the remainder of the gully in a twinkling. A charge of dynamite placed in the right position might make this the 'gulley of gullies'.

C Petrie, 25 September 1950

Called in here 11.40 en route for a snow climb up the front of the Devil's Point. Made a successful attempt on the Douglas Gully of Lochnagar under excellent snow conditions on Friday 28th – First Winter Ascent.

DG Leslie and TW Patey, 30 December 1950

Someone has added:

NICE WORK, TOM! BLOODY GOOD!

The Douglas-Gibson Gully on Lochnagar was a long-standing problem that had defeated many parties since Douglas and Gibson's first attempt in 1893. It was first climbed in summer conditions in 'rubbers' in 1933 by C. Ludwig, who described his ascent as 'perhaps unjustifiable'. Here, in a Corrour Bothy visitors' book, almost in passing, is the first record of the first winter ascent. As later described in more detail in CCJ No 87, 1950–1, its final section required using an ice axe as a foothold and tunnelling through an exit cornice that projected for 25ft.

It signified a new era in Scottish winter climbing.

'The Edge', Cameron McNeish, 1994

Arrived at the bothy from Garbh Coire after a night in a tent at 3,400ft. The tent was sunk in a two-foot ditch in the snow but no blizzard arose to test the efficiency of the equipment; condensation gave a little trouble. Before leaving the corrie, Braeriach was ascended by the Central and Eastern Gullies, and good glissading was found in the Western Gully.

P McGovern and Iain Smart, 30 December 1950

Glorious morning. Bright sun. Tent dug out with great difficulty in spite of thaw, then draped it over bothy roof securely belayed to chimney. Finally made a record late start and attacked the ice slope above hut on the cliff of Devil's Point. Time prevented completion so traversed off and reached summit via shoulder.

E Walker (Miss), 29 March 1951

Tackled Crown Buttress (*Garbh Choire Mor*), which was covered in powder snow and pretty icy. We followed Winram's 1950 route up ribs and past a large block to a groove on the right. The loose snow made the groove exceedingly difficult and ice in the final vertical section stopped us. We descended 40ft and were forced under the 'crown' and on to a vertical impasse on the right. However, Richards got us out of difficulty by a beautiful balance lead across a near-vertical wall to a safe 'sentry box'. Very steep rock led directly up on small holds to a final crack (20ft), also iced and pretty severe.

The latter half of this climb is a first ascent and the whole of it a first winter ascent (we think). Nevertheless, none of us wishes to repeat it. Time 5½ hours, 450ft.

RB Richards, John Gadd and Ken James (Climbers' Club),
24 November 1951

The buttress was named for the rock formation at its top. The 'crown' itself was first climbed in winter in 1967 (Grade III).

Woke to find that we were members of a search party. We were preparing to leave when the lost party was found.

Kenneth R Petrie, 22 July 1952

Arrived 5.15pm from Luibeg on skis in a blizzard – we were disappointed to see the depth of soft snow as we had hopes of a climb tomorrow – but conditions do not appear to be too good, although excellent for skiing.

[The following day] Today the snow was still soft and a thaw had set in, so the morning was spent skiing up on Coire Odhar, where conditions were quite good. As we are leaving now for Luibeg (3pm)

we take this opportunity to wish all future visitors to the bothy a
very happy and prosperous New Year.

A Graham Nicol, 29–30 December 1952

Climbed rib between Domed Ridge and West Gully, Coire Bhrochain,
300ft. Just Diff. owing to loose rock and some vegetation. Took
rightmost of two ribs separated by slabby depression. Then a long
shelf of slabs under the right-hand gable to a pinnacle and back above a
vegetable pitch. Slabs and a chokestone chimney finished the climb to
the left of the upper very steep wall. Poor climb but looks magnificent
from corrie floor.

R Winram, C Petrie and M Smith, 28 June 1953

Mac Smith and Kenny Winram were central figures in the
fraternity of pioneering 1950s north-east climbers. To reach the
Cairngorms, along with Tom Patey and others, they would share
petrol costs with Adam Watson, who owned a jeep that could take
six passengers plus rucksacks.

Arrived from Pools of Dee camp at 14.30. Cpt Dietz and Mr Davidson
climbed on Devil's Point, meeting Messrs Winkelstein and Barwinkle,
two distinguished Alpinists from Munich, on the summit. Wooding detail
to Derry Lodge area, returned 7.30pm bringing firewood. 14 bodies and
1 dog slept here.

[The following day] Main party left with full kit to climb over Cairn
Toul & Braeriach to ski hut at Rothiemurchus. August 26 Cpt Dietz
R.A.E.C. (with four sergeants and Mr Davidson). Rear party left at 13.30
to return via Pools of Dee to ski hut, collecting food.

Mr Anholt (with two sergeants), 26 August 1953

[Sunday] Left Derry Lodge. Up Glen Derry to Loch Etchachan,
which is frozen over. Brilliant sunshine with short snow showers.
The snow is deep, dry and hard on the tops and snow bridges
reliable. Crossed to Loch Avon (frozen), where more wondrous
sights present. Kicked steps down, cleared snow and ice from under
the Shelter Stone and set off for Forefinger Pinnacle. The steps
became very hard to kick towards the top and I developed cramp.
This was rather alarming as the final 25ft above the pinnacle were

impassable. However we returned safely to the loch to find two more medics established. Cleared snow out.

[Monday] We climbed out at the head of Loch Avon, keeping dry and warm in frozen snow. Faced a blizzard across Macdhui. We got very wet getting to the bothy.

[Tuesday] Set off up Devil's Point (north face) at 7.30am. Dry and hot. Snow and mist came down after we had feasted on the sun-bathed view. Went round by Cairn Toul, Wells of Dee and Braeriach, with brilliant views when the mist cleared at intervals. Part scrambled, part glissaded down to the Lairig. Again got very wet returning.

[Wednesday] Back to Derry Lodge, regretfully, and to Leeds. PS Found a scarf near the Wells of Dee. This we leave here and hope that its owner may have the pleasure of reclaiming it.

29 March 1954

[Sunday] Arrived from Luibeg 6.30pm to be welcomed by four very nice young ladies. A pleasant first night was enjoyed.

[Monday] A foul day – climbed Braeriach by Campion Gully (*Coire Bhrochain*) first winter ascent (?), poor conditions, only the cornice giving difficulty.

[Tuesday] Excellent day for first winter ascent of Chokestone Gully (Angel's Peak) in good hard snow. A severe ice pitch was encountered. Continued over Cairn Toul and Devil's Point in perfect conditions.

[Wednesday] No definite climbs were left worth doing in our opinion (Bhrochain Slabs is artificial under present conditions), so spent an enjoyable day hillwalking in fine weather. Ben Macdhui, Cairn Gorm, Cairn Lochan, Ben Macdhui, Cairn a' Mhaim, bothy.

5 April 1954

With no dedicated guidebooks to climbing in the Cairngorms, it is understandable that some climbers would be unaware of previous ascents. Chokestone Gully was in fact first climbed in winter in 1937, when the final chockstone pitch was a wall of sheer ice (Grade III).

Apologise for the state of the bothy. Unfortunately there was an accident in the corrie next to Lochan Uaine last night when two

climbers fell from Chokestone Gully. The mountain rescue squad
was called and the whole night was spent in coming and going in
dreadful weather.

Anne Ingram, 13 April 1954

Contoured round cliffs from Lochan Uaine outflow to Chimney
Pot in Garbh Coire Dhaidh. Depth of 'randkluft' at foot of Sphinx
estimated 15–20ft. Snowfield in ideal condition for glissading 'sans
piolet' – two-inch melt surface above snow-ice – christie turns pure
delight. No crevasses yet. Field 250ft in length below Pinnacles and
unbroken from Devil's to Apron Gullies.

Evidence of June cloudburst not so marked here as further north
and west, ie gravel runnels in Lairig north of Pools, high water
diffusion in Nethy and Am Beanaidh, split course of Beanaidh Bheag,
much torn-up heaps of stream-bed boulders and non-established
bridge, but gravel washed from the cliffs was seen on the snow,
forming mounds of ice through delaying melt and evaporation.

M Smith, 20 July 1956

The 'randkluft' (German) is the gap between the snowfield and
the adjacent rock face at its back. 'Sans piolet' (French) means
'without an ice axe'.

Broke all personal records by rising at 4.00am and leaving the bothy
at 5.30am. The intention was to see the sunrise from the summit of
Ben Macdhui, but we were almost an hour too late, arriving at the
summit at 7.30am. Snow conditions in the corrie were excellent.
We cut steps up the last part of the ascent. Glorious morning, and
we felt our virtue in early rising richly rewarded!

[The following day] We intended to rise at 3.00am to make sure
of seeing the sunrise from Ben Macdhui but we overslept by 4½ hours.
We packed and left for the Steall Hut (*Glen Nevis*).

John Sutton, 22 March 1959

In April 1962, Adam Watson, using cross-country skis, skied over
Ben Avon & Beinn a' Bhuird, crossed Glen Derry, skied over Ben
Macdui and Cairn Gorm, crossed the Lairig Ghru, skied over Braeriach to Cain Toul and descended to Corrour. The 38 miles (34 on skis)
and 8,700ft of climbing took 16 hours.

It was good to warm up again gliding quickly down the moraines to Corrour Bothy, where I took off my skis to go inside. The last sun rays were burning red on Ben Macdui. By contrast the bothy was dark and gloomy, and I was feeling not at all tired, so I moved on [to Luibeg and Derry Lodge].

Adam Watson, SMCJ No 27, 1963

On one night in 1966, Scottish and English climbers shared the bothy.

Scottish entry –

Set off for Garbh Coire Mor at 0800 hrs along the River Dee, which was solid ice. Greg and John decided to try Egyptian Fantasy. Gave up 25ft from cornice owing to vertical and overhanging fresh snow. Raymond, Eric and Doug did Solo Gully (1st winter ascent) and Raymond took 1½ hours to surmount the cornice. Doug was hauled up next and succeeded in ruining all the steps from the last belay to the cornice.

Eric decided to peel off. He met Greg and John, who were retreating from Egyptian Fantasy, and they all returned to the bothy by the Dee again. Raymond and Doug went to the top of Cairn Toul and returned 2 hours after the rest at 1900 hrs. John made some popcorn – and ate most of it himself. 3 Englishmen here – we've no prejudice.

Eric Henry, 4 April 1966

Someone has challenged the account of Solo Gully by changing '1st winter ascent' to '3rd winter ascent'.

English entry –

After surmounting great difficulties we arrived at the bothy in time to make a pot of tea. After tea we ascended Devil's Point. On the ascent we watched the quaint old custom of the Scots sliding down the hill on plastic bags. Returned to the bothy to find it full of Scots (11 in fact).

Made ascent of Ben Macdhui and claimed it for England. Ascent quite interesting with ice near the top. Descended by stream and practised glissading, and then how to stop after falling. Returned

to bothy and put on duvets as we are not used to these severe
Scottish winters.

Roger Payne (and two English companions), 4 April 1966

Scottish entry –

The Englishmen have just returned after being up Macdui. They are all
freezing (obviously not used to the mild Scots winter).

Eric Henry, 4 April 1966

The day is foul, needless to say. Steady rain at all times. Even a
suspicion of snow higher bloody up. We are spending a pleasant
day here at Corrour getting fit for the Alps in July. As Rébuffat
says, with climbing it is not so much a question of physical balance
as mental balance. It is very peaceful here at Corrour (during the
day). Someone has just made a decision to go out. Hope he goes far
enough...

Our guilt over festering built up to a critical value and around 2pm
we upped and went intrepidly out in the rain in the direction of the
March Burn. I was less reluctant to embark on this foolhardy venture
than the others because I had just purchased a giant-sized cagoule
from that paragon of all mountain equipment specialists – Graham
Tiso of Edinburgh. Maybe one day we will achieve sufficient mental
balance to fester entirely without guilt.

Today made it obvious we must put in a lot of hard festering
before we go to the Alps. We climbed up to the top of Ben Macdhui
by the most direct route. On top there was 6 inches of new snow. In
places old snow as deep as 6ft abounded. Of course, foolishly thinking
that summer might mean something in Scotland, we left snow gaiters
and ice axes at home. At the top I left the others and ploughed off in
a complete whiteout to the top of Coire Sputan Dearg.

All this time I couldn't see a bloody thing. One of the others, a
Scotsman, told me that Scotland only has three seasons – spring,
autumn, winter. Why is it that I've never seen the view from
Macdhui? I'm being persecuted in some subtle way. All week it is fine
then over the weekend it is foul. It has happened so often now it has
gone beyond reasonable statistical likelihood.

21 May 1966

Gaston Rébuffat (1921–85) was a renowned French alpinist and guide. Among other achievements, he was the first to climb the six great north faces of the Alps. The format of his book *Le Massif des Écrins: Les 100 Belles Courses et Randonnées* inspired my first guidebook, *100 Best Routes on Scottish Mountains*, in 1987.

[In heavy rain] Climbed Domed Rib solo using combined breaststroke and freestyle technique.

Douglas S Cameron, 13 July 1966

I will now give my account of that horrible 13th July. This tale of human endurance and suffering should not be read by children or by those of a nervous disposition. The wind had died down to a gale force ten and the amount of rain had dropped to a mere three inches an hour...

After swimming across the corrie (Coire Bhrochain) we made our way to the towering masses of smooth granite of Pisa (Diff), shedding 1½ pints of cold sweat. I overcame the 1st pitch. Then I brought up Alan who started to swim the 2nd pitch. However, due to the law of gravity, the guidebook fell out of his pocket and it plunged into the black depths of the corrie.

Further epics occurred – I shall not go into details. The last few pitches were overhanging scree slopes, but we made it (minus much skin and sweat). Alan (wisely) decided to go to the summit of Braeriach. The rest of us wanted more, so we galloped down to Coire Bhrochain.

After crossing some snow we arrived at our route: Domed Ridge. After climbing 200ft of overhanging moss Norman and myself roped up while Doug went on and was enveloped in swirling mist and rain. We lost the route and ended up on long severe pitches. There was an acute shortage of belays but we managed with the use of moss jug-handles.

By now I was having trouble breathing because of the rain that entered by ears, nostrils and mouth (an aqualung is very advisable on this climb). I was miserable. The hailstones came down in pailfuls, filling all the holds. After nearly peeling, I got to the top.

We ran along the top to touch the cairn (Braeriach) then made a
hasty retreat... and made good time down to the Lairig Ghru path.
I crossed the Dee (harder than the climbs we had done), now in
spate. Victorious, we collapsed into the bothy. After stripping off we
had something to eat... Finally we rolled into our sleeping bags and
so ended the 13th of July.

Brian Dunn, 14 July 1966

Corrour today continues to provide a base for climbing on the
surrounding peaks, but its popularity as a base for major rock and
ice routes has waned since the 1960s. The existing visitors' books
of the 1970s and onwards record no climbing exploits to match
those of earlier decades.

It is no wonder that the pre-war pioneers found the newly open
bothy the perfect base for exploration.

> The early mountaineers, who revelled in the false security of gul-
> lies and chimneys and spurned the hazardous freedom of the open
> face, must have found the Cairngorms a veritable Mecca.
>
> Tom Patey, *One Man's Mountains*, 1971

Tom preferred the wide-open spaces of rock faces and in the
1950s, with improved gear, he led the way in pioneering a whole
new class of rock and ice climbs – 'a weekly harvest of new
routes'. As he wrote, 'In snow and ice climbing, the Cairngorms
and Lochnagar yield to none.' Adam Watson recalled an evening in
1954 when, after exploration on various Lairig Ghru crags, various
parties assembled at Corrour for an evening of music and singing
to Tom's accordion.

> All the bothies were well patronised – Luibeg, Lochend, Gelder
> Shiel, Bynack, the Geldie Bothies, Altanour, Corrour and of course
> the Shelter Stone.
>
> Tom Patey, *One Man's Mountains*, 1971

But by the 1960s Corrour was beginning to fall out of favour
amongst the climbing fraternity. For those who wanted a base even
nearer to the climbs in An Garbh Choire, the Lairig Club built an
alternative ramshackle refuge there in 1966 (NN 959986). Never
more than an increasingly dilapidated structure, after a campaign

by Neil Reid and Kenny Freeman it was entrusted to the care of the MBA and renovated in 2018. With a stone covering over a small steel frame, barely big enough to stand upright in, it remains more of an emergency shelter than a bothy.

For a more congenial base, the climbers of the 50s preferred the camaraderie of the motley crew who gathered at keeper Bob Scott's Bothy at Luibeg near Derry Lodge. Tom Patey recalled a tale of the 'hairy vagabond' known as the 'Birmingham Highlander'.

> This gentleman wore his kilt in the manner of his professedly Highland ancestors, ie *in modo naturae*. He took pains to advertise this, and it was therefore all the more fitting that it should have led to his undoing. One day when walking near the lip of a steep snowfield, he lost his footing and set off upon a long involuntary sitting glissade. Most of us were aware of the heat that can be generated through thick corduroy trousers. This gentleman had no such protection. He has not been seen around much lately.
>
> Tom Patey, *One Man's Mountains*, 1971

But the main factor that ended Corrour's tenure as a climbers' refuge was a desire for new horizons. By the mid-1950s all the main lines in the Lairig Ghru had been climbed and the new tigers of the day had moved on to greater challenges on the towering crags of Lochnagar, the Loch Avon Basin and the great corries of the Eastern Cairngorms.

Today, Corrour is more a base and staging post for walkers.

RIDING TO CORROUR

IT MAY SURPRISE many who walk the rugged paths to Corrour that there is a long history of taking bicycles through the Lairig Ghru. Whether this amounts to 'cycling' is open to debate.

> But the idea of walking – from Ballater to Braemar, or even from Braemar to Inverey! By most people, apparently, it would be dismissed as supremely ridiculous. Nobody seems to walk nowadays. The ubiquitous bicycle has penetrated even to these remote regions; and I and my companion, who have not yet succumbed to the ruling passion, are regarded as 'cranks' – two eccentric individuals obstinately adhering to a quite exploded form of locomotion.
>
> Robert Anderson, 'A Fortnight at Inverey', CCJ No 18, 1902

Nevertheless, the first SMC guidebook to the Cairngorms left cyclists with no illusions about what they were in for.

> A bicycle cannot be used with any advantage on this route [the Lairig Ghru] as the going almost all the way is very rough and the machine cannot even be wheeled on the path.
>
> Henry Alexander, 'SMC Guidebook: The Cairngorms', 1928

Cycling from Dundee to Aviemore. Men are certified insane for less than this.

> 29 June 1929

Alex (Sandy) Tewnion and companion, two self-proclaimed 'tyros', decided to tackle the Lairig Ghru by bicycle in 1937, as Sandy later recalled after the war.

> Slipping on rolling pebbles, squelching through bogs and mud and drenched with perspiration. we struggled on... On we plodded, sometimes carrying the cycles 100 yards at a stretch over

stony patches of ground, again pushing them through running
water where the path degenerated to a stream.

...

Across the Dee appeared a small stone house, a tall figure in a kilt
giving a friendly wave as we passed lugging our heavy machines.
We returned his gesture and debated as to who would stay in
such a lonely spot, but the mystery was solved for us a short
distance along, when two men came in sight, bent double under
enormous packs. [*They explained that*] 'this is Glen Dee; yonder
is Carrar (Corrour) Bothy, where we're staying for a few days;
and up there is the Devil's Point, where we'll be climbing tomorrow if the weather holds.'

They camped overnight in a storm then continued.

Climbing, ever climbing, the bicycles bouncing on stones or sticking
in pools of mud, we squelched and floundered on to the north.

They eventually stashed their packs to manhandle the bicycles
over the summit of the pass before returning to retrieve the packs
on foot. Despite their privations, after reaching Aviemore they
made...

...a solemn vow to the giant Cairngorms: 'We shall soon
return'.

And we did; and despite some game legs and wives and such like
acquired during the war, we still do.
            Alex Tewnion, 'Over the Lairig Ghru', CCJ No85, 1946–7

Sandy went on to become a stalwart of the Cairngorm Club
who would revisit Corrour many times. In 1941, he made the first
ascent of Pinnacle Buttress in Garbh Choire Mor with his brother
Sydney. He was injured in Normandy in 1944 and told he would
never walk the hills again, but he persevered with a walking stick
until he could. In 1950, he helped in the renovation of Corrour.
Tragically, Sydney died in a storm while walking to Benalder Cottage from the other Corrour near Loch Ossian.

Arrived today from Aviemore... Accompanied a girl most of the way,
she going on to Inverey. Being gentlemen (?) we carried her cycle this

far, for which she was very grateful. First instance I've heard of a girl
cyclist tackling this on her own.

J Ramsay, 28 May 1939

Joe Thompson of Preston Lancs and his bike Horace called here to cook a
meal. (Horace was left on the other side of the stream).
Over the Lairig from Inverey I will take my bike,
Even if most of the way I will have to hike.

Joe Thompson, 18 June 1956

Simon (the mad mountain cyclist), Braemar to Aviemore, stopped for
lunch. The bicycle is finding it tough – weather, stony going, down to
the axles in some peaty bits. The porridge is bubbling, so bye for now.

Simon, 11 November 1981

'Cycling' the Glen Feshie – Lairig Ghru loop. Not the weather for it today.

Brian Watson, 18 October 1984

The following visitor noted:

Yes, this chap really was 'cycling', although when I met him he was
having a slight problem on the scree by the Pools of Dee.

18 October 1984

Cycled to Derry Lodge then humphed it to here.

John Watson and Walker McArthur, 6 August 1996

Did a circuit from Linn of Dee to Derry Lodge to here – to White
Bridge, to home again. Brought my bike. Big mistake. I'm knackered.
Must be back by 5pm. Think I may be late.

S Heyes, 5 September 1996

Cycled in to Luibeg Bridge, ditched the bike, walked on to summit
of Carn a' Mhaim. Will doss down here overnight and bag Cairn Toul
and Angel's Peak tomorrow (if John's snoring doesn't collapse the
walls onto us during the night). Then walk back out.

Willie Thomson and John Hands, 28 December 1997

Should obviously have been here yesterday due to weather, but then
some of us have to work! Biked to end of track from Linn of Dee
(must buy a more comfortable saddle).

Angus Pollie, 19 June 1998

Today, with a Land Rover track from Linn of Dee to Derry Lodge and an improved path from there to Luibeg Bridge, mountain biking has become an increasingly popular way of reducing the walk-in to Corrour.

When the National Trust for Scotland bought Mar Lodge Estate in 1995, the Easter Charitable Trust's substantial monetary contribution to the purchase required that 'NTS shall make continuous and constant efforts to dissuade, and where possible to prohibit, the use of mechanical or wheeled vehicles'. The NTS duly erected signs to actively discourage bicycle access, although without actually prohibiting it.

This policy was revised in 2001 to allow bicycle access as far as the NTS could drive its Land Rovers. This new policy was itself overturned by the Land Reform (Scotland) Act (2003) and accompanying Scottish Outdoor Access Code (2005), which gives a statutory right of responsible access for outdoor recreation. Importantly, it does not distinguish between access on foot, bicycle or horse. There are now no signs that discourage bicycle access.

FRIENDS FROM ABROAD

UNTIL AFTER THE Second World War, visitors to Corrour were almost universally from Great Britain. Improved travel opportunities since then have seen increasing numbers of foreign visitors, mostly from Western Europe but increasingly from all around the world.

Two French went here on this day and meet here sympathetic 'Ecossais' singing, dancing and playing bag-pipe (without bag). I took here my first lesson of dance. I was not a good pupil.

Paulette Confais, 27 July 1950

Après 5 heures de marche dans le vent, la pluie, la brume et la semi-obscurité...
   Arriveé ici dans la nuit (10.30pm), nous y avons trouvé l'acceuil sympathique de toute une bande d'Ecossais bruyants et joyeux.

3 Parisiens, 31 July 1950

The Ecossais added:

Having splashed our way in mist and rain over a bog-ridden path for 5 hours, the sight of the bothy's bright roof (following the 1950 renovation) was indeed welcome. We were joined late at night by above three Parisiens and a very jolly night was passed with French and Scots songs.

31 July 1950

These Wee Scotch Midges certainly have a voracious appetite.

Vicente Llinares, 13 August 1950

Yesterday we came here and met with a man who had lost his way in the mist. He was very thankful and said we had saved his life... We passed all three the night here. He had as cover our tent, for blankets

198

are not in this bothy. However, it is very good that here is a bothy in the mountains. We spent here a cosy evening and slept very well.

We are two thankful Dutch boys, 19 August 1955

The first existing post-war German entry in the visitors' books:

Here is a fine youth hostel without any duty. FURCHTLOS UND TREU (Fearless and True)

24 August 1955

Having walked, waded and climbed my way half through three continents I can confidently compare the Cairngorm peaks with the Dolomites, your fine Cairngorm plateau with the Jos plateau in Africa or the Gunong Tahan range in Malaya, this fine silver sand with the more dun-coloured product of the Sahara or the grey wastes of the Arabian Hadramaut. But there is one alone beyond compare – the Dee, and in particular the coldness thereof. I have never, never, NEVER had such cold feet as I had half an hour ago in the Dee, No, never. But blessings upon you and peace for the use of this fine bothy.

JG Wallis, Nigeria, 18 May 1956

Not as sunny as in Spain but smashing in its beauty and grandeur.
PS Found waterproof trousers half-way round from Braeriach to Cairn Toul. Resisted temptation and left them here for owner to claim.

Carlos, Barcelona, 30 June 1956

Dr John Black and 34 Swedish scouts arrived here from Luibeg, made a cup of tea, and then returned to Luibeg, some via Carn a' Mhaim, some via the Devil's Point and Glen Geusachan.

28 July 1957

A German living on oats and rice came and went.

5 August 1957

A German and a Scottish boy joined to walk from Aviemore to Braemar together. Arrived here last night almost killed by the midges and the feet wet by walking through 'damned bloody' bogs. Nevertheless, a wonderful countryside around here.

Wolf (Berlin), 17 August 1957

Had fine weather on Ben Macdhui and could see Ben Nevis some 68 miles off. There's a fine fire of heather here tonight and a fine crew of English fellows, 2 Scots and 1 American. This place is blazin'.

Stephen Hoyt, Washington, USA, 28 July 1966

Two Yanks making their way through the Lairig Ghru on Independence Day. Mice aren't so bad, once you get to know them.

Rich and Susan Welsh, 4 July 1970

Il pleut, il fait froid et il vente. La montagne est magnifique.

Stéphane, 15 July1970

Nuit memorable! 22 dans cette cabane. Les places sont chère.

Brigitte Maillet, 16 July 1970

Scotland is a beautiful country and especially these mountains.

A Yank from the state of Washington, 13 October 1970

Spent my last night in Scotland in the bothy. Walking through the mountains and sleeping in an unknown bothy is a thrill. Hope more Dutchmen will find time to do something like this.

15 October 1970

Couldn't sleep due to an old Englishman who couldn't sleep because of mice.

Fritz and Tina (Holland), 20 June 1972

With my friend Reiner Bertram I arrived at 3.00pm. The weather was not good. It was very long raining and much fog.

Wolfgang Sippol, West Germany, 23 July 1972

A wee b------ of a descent from Ben Macdui, boulder-hopping with wet blistered feet. But pain and suffering are good for you. One comes into the mountains to torture oneself stupid; isn't that right, Hamish?... Most impressed with the Cairngorm hills but they really need vast areas of impenetrable scrub to make walking absolute hell, such as it is in the SW of Tassie.

Dick Williams, Australia, 23 August 1979

Schottland überhauft super. Es hat die schönste Landschaft die es überhauft gibt, denke ich wenigstens.

Peter Ingenbleek, West Germany, 20 July 1982

Fantastic sunny morning. If you are interested in diffusion of polarised light you can always email me at...

Jan Popelek, Czechoslovakia, 26 June 1996

Is lovely place, especially after long day in hills. Scotland is lovely country. Verry [sic] beautiful. Big climbs, thow. Verry hard. Will come back soon.

Hans, Germany, 30 June 1996

We were forced by the rain to put up our tent about 4 kilometres north from here. It was stormy and we feared the tent might be blown away or the River Dee might rise enough to let us swim away. Right here, this hut seems to me like heaven on earth.

Flo 'wet shoes' Jager, Germany, 5 July 1996

Walked up from Braemar yesterday. Quite a hike, and we haven't reached the summit yet. Lovely country – quite similar to the Barren Grounds in Northern Canada, except that we don't have the peaks nor nearly as much heather, and caribou instead of deer.

Brenda McNair from Yellowknife, Northwest Territories, Canada, 1 August 1996

There are midges, rain and mice.
That is nice.

Berndi, Germany, 9 August 1996

After many 'bad weather days' it is a wonderful day today. The sky is clear! For us these are the last days of our vacation (holliday) [sic]. For the first time this holiday we have swimmed (sorry swam). We found a wonderfull [sic] waterfall to do that. The Dee was almost 'warm'. And we found a deer gewei [antler]. Sorry for the bad English. Greetings.

Kathrin and Stefan, Netherlands, 10 July 1997

Walking in the glen this evening, headed towards the bothy, I was reminded once again of the restorative power of nature. The sun had long since dipped behind the hills, but the afterglow reflected off the clouds and illuminated the valley below. The deer in the stream took little notice of me, accepting me as part of this place, and I walked along feeling wondrous and lit up all inside.

The walk-in reminded me a bit of the start of the Copeland Track
in New Zealand, which winds its way towards Mount Cook for
several kilometres before turning left and going up over the Southern
Alps to begin a 33-kilometre descent towards the Tasman Sea.
There's a hut at the base of the mountains there, too, and as was the
case tonight, I found it empty. Solitude: in an area as popular as this it
shouldn't be taken lightly.

I've been on a two-week climbing holiday that took me up the
west coast of Scotland, to Orkney and Shetland, and now I'm slowly
working my way south. I have to be back at work on Sunday, to
be followed by a 3-month tour in Bosnia, but my memories of the
Highlands will keep me sane until I get back next spring.

Jamie, USA, 21 August 1997

Came here by 1200 after gotten stuck in bad weather at the Iron
Bridge 1hr after Aviemore. Actually I wanted to stay here for two
days before going to Hull to get my ferry. But here is only place for
one – that's me or the midges. But unfortunately I can't make the
midges move away. So it is a little bit like surrender because I do go
tomorrow. I am really happy to get away from this winged driven
command. Only dead midges are good midges.

Schulz (Germany), 14 August 1997

Paysage sauvage et rude climat. Vive les cols enneigés et les lagopèdes
[ptarmigan] d'Ecosse. Quel Plaisir de se réveiller, sous ce toit, avec des
volutes de vapeur d'eau au dessus de sa tête.

Arnaud et Emmanuelle, France, 10 November 1997

I am in a bothy and it is warm. Outside is cold. All hail bothies
everywhere. We are climbing the Lairig Ghru today. I am excited.
ROCKS. BOULDERS. It was Independence Day two days ago.

Love from Susan Greig, USA, 6 July 1998

A little joke: it is summer! We were told to walk from Aviemore/Loch
Morlich to Blair Atholl, but we didn't know we had to swim plenty of
rivers. Now we are lucky that this little nice house was built before
19th July 1998. Now hot soup is saving our lives. Let's hope there is
no snow outside tomorrow morning because we have no skis with
us. However, we all love Scotland. It must be boring in sunshine and

blue sky, so we cannot complain about some water drops falling from the sky. But we enjoy drying our clothes.

Venture Scout Group 11, Vienna, Austria, 19 July 1998

Scotland has been brilliant. Strawberry picking in Laurencekirk, grouse beating in Kingussie, Cairngorms walkabout for 4 days, who knows what else…

Chris Dipnisio, New Jersey, USA, 25 September 1998

A German guy, a Swiss guy and an Israeli guy were walking in the Cairngorms. That's the beginning of a big joke… but I don't know how to finish.

Swiss guy, 3 April 2016

I say that the volunteers of the MBA are wonderful people and need all the support they can get… But when I look at the walls and ceiling I can almost cry when I see the writings and carvings of dates and names who stayed here. I think for that purpose there is a guest book, but some think they can use it to burn!! What would these people think and do when they have guests in their houses and these guests start to carve their names in doors and write on the wall? When I am back in Holland I will donate to the MBA and I hope everybody will do so!! Enjoy your stay. Love and peace for all.

Richard Knutsen, Holland, 2 May 2016

Fantastic bothy. People should care more about such precious places.

[illegible], Germany, 9 June 2016

We stopped for lunch on the way from Bob Scott's bothy to Aviemore. Can't miss the chance to see 'Penis of the Devil' from close.

Bara & Leuka, 28 June 2016

3 Czechs came from Braemar and were thankful for all goods of boothie [sic].

Tomas, Petr & Ludvic, 12 May 2019

Today I walked from Linn of Dee with my cousin Samuel. I have been in Scotland for 6 weeks and I'm enjoying the amazing views. I'm from Tasmania and, although the views in Tas are similar, I have been able to relax and truly take them in here. Bothys are very sweet. I love to meet

people here and exchange stories. I hope everyone here gets the chance
to stay in a bothy in Tas. There are plenty of littler huts close to Hobart
on Mount Wellington. I have not yet stayed in one, but staying here
makes me want to go and stay in one back home. Let's help keep these
places wild. Keep Tassie Wild. All the best.

Marlee, 5 June 2019

Also in 2019, Braemar Mountain Rescue Team was called out
when three Polish walkers used a mobile phone to call 999 after
reaching Corrour.

The trio… had parked their car in Aviemore and made the round
trip to the bothy. However, they were unfamiliar with the hills and
it took them double the length of time an experienced walker would
take. They were taken to the team's base in Braemar and eventually
they were given a lift back to Aviemore.

The Press and Journal, Aberdeen, 8 April 2019

This incident proves not only the continuing importance of Corrour in mountain safety but also the increasing impact of instant
communication since the early days of its life as a bothy.

A FUNNY THING HAPPENED

HUMOUR IS NEVER in short supply when staying at Corrour.

If Shelley, Byron, Keats or Gray
Should read these doggerel verses
They'd rise from out their honoured graves
And kick your b----y erses.

14 July 1931

Corrour! Scotland's greatest hospitalitary edifice,
A veritable ambulatory huskie's paradise,
Beloved by all who humped big packs across the passes,
And considered by the masses – as silly asses.

KR Nielson, successor to McGonagall (of Dundee),
18 July 1931

Oh for a minister to save my sole,
It's parting company with my boot.

18 July 1938

Tonight we have a fire. A magnificent fire. In its fiercest moments
it has driven us to the back of the bothy. Even Jim, the Asbestos
Wonder, was driven before its power. Shirts have been abandoned
and even the door has been opened to temper the boiler-room
atmosphere. The 'Old Boys' are suffering with burned knees. Phew!

Jimmie Wyne (Creag Dhu), 5 January 1938

There was a young lady of Ballater
Who went for a dip in Loch Callater
Her natatory prowess
She started to showess
Then up came a monster and Swallater.

James S Robertson, 24 September 1938

At the moment there are 5 of us, but the weakest will probably
succumb before morning and the bodies will make fine seats and
provide food for the survivors.

I January 1939

Came over the pass today with a Londoner who told me in course
of conversation that the Lairig Ghru is the finest pass in England. He
made several remarks equally blasphemous and was lucky to get past
this place alive.

James Cunningham, 30 May 1939

Pity we can't stay another day, when the scarf Bill is knitting would be
big enough to re-roof the bothy.

25 September 1939

The roof may leak
(It could be worse),
But still it's better
Than this 'ere verse.

Anne Balmain, 18 September 1949

Here we sit, two ravishing females,
With jackets, trousers and hoods,
Oh! How we long for the sight of two he-males.
Boy, would it make us feel good.

Jean Stephen, 20, and Marjorie Jones, 20,
(addresses provided), 13 October 1949

'Night on a Bare Mountain' has nothing on this. Country a bit too
barren for me, looking forward to seeing trees again. Would have felt
better if one of those 3cwt boulders hadn't taken away half my left leg.
Another thing which made life more miserable was a herd of haggis
which set on us. Thank goodness Leo laughed – they couldn't stand
that and withdrew, leaving two of their number sizzling on the log.

Bob Davies, 6 August 1951

Oh the grand old duke of York,
He had ten thousand men.

He marched them up the Lairig Ghru
And he marched them doon agin.

An' when they were up they were wet
An' when they were doon they were glad
An' when they were only half-way up it is more than likely that they
were brewing tea in Corrour Bothy

Ancient Sassenach marching song

3 August 1952

There was a young lady from Spain,
Who when climbing the Cairngorms in rain,
Would first climb the peaks
Than strip off her breeks,
And shout 'I'm insane, I'm insane'.

R Rochester, 14 August 1956

For Sale: Corrour Bothy. Spacious residential apartment. Antique
out-of-town flat, ideal for bachelor or young married couple, retired
gentry or teachers. Lying in its own heather garden (founded 3 million
years BC), this desirable residence has much to offer. Over 50 lighting
points, built-in furniture, genuine Highland home floor. Many artistic
pre-Reformation frescoes. Many infamous people scribed their name
on the spacious craftsman-built roof. Running water. Private access
road. Small hill at back ideal for young children or old age pensioner.
Price £6,000 o.n.o.

Alexander Shand, 4 April 1966

Having eventually got a magnificent fire going, a Czechoslovakian
gentleman of unknown parentage set about extinguishing it by drying
all his gear.

5 August 1966

The instructor spent the night mastering the art of balancing, while
half-asleep, along the rung of his li-lo, with the feet of two churls ready
to stamp in his ribs if he move forward and – at a guess – the bottom
of a young lady ready to administer a *coup de grâce* if he move back.

Glenmore party, 5 August 1966

Wanted – Haggis Beaters. Assemble on top of Cairn Toul at 2am to
be issued with orders. Prospective beaters should be able to hit a
haggis at 40 yards with a loaded kilt.

20 August 1966

Double-headed haggis hunting. Followed tracks on Cairn Toul to
Einich Cairn, then cloud came down and we followed haggis down
wrong side. Got back to bothy empty-haggised.

D MacCain, 22 August 1966

Having had a meander up from Derry, we decided it was too wet to
go any further, so we are returning to Derry.

Margaret Cruse with Dennis Jack, 19 June 1972
(Dennis just came for a sly look at Playboy)

Caruthers and I are exhausted. After 9 weeks in the hills wearing
only ski caps and carpet slippers the frostbite is excruciating... I fear
for my own sanity and suppose that dear Maria and the little ones
will never see their dear Papa again. Already Caruthers has tried to
stumble off into the blizzard. Such was his suicidal frenzy that he left
behind his slippers and wore only his balaclava. Must sign off now. I've
got to eat this pen.

Captain Scott, aka Donny O'Rourke, 2 July 1977

Have just spent an enjoyable night listening to my splendid collection
of albums. Had no trouble with the generator but had some trouble
with the alignment of the speakers. Must say the coral cartridge
performed excellently on the Linn Sondek LP12, and in comparison
with the Ariston RD11S proved excellent with no sign of upper
harmonic distortion and very clean vocals. Managed to compensate
for the reverberant bothy's acoustics with my graphic equaliser (glad
I managed to slip it into an empty pocket next to the wine bottles)
and the bothy's walls seemed to cope admirably with the generous
200 watts per channel 'eased' out by the amplifier. Apart from
complaints from some nearby residents in Braemar, had no trouble
with the system.

20 July 1980

Hillwalking is like sex:
Some of it's pleasure, some of it's pain.

When the pain brings the pleasure
We come again.

JR Ewing, Gourock not Dallas, 24 August 1980

0930. Somebody has managed to force the door open with an ice axe. Suppose we shall now have to get up. (I believe this is what is called an Alpine start.)

30 December 1982

What a frightful place. No heating. No lighting. Nothing but cold concrete walls. You would think the I would do something about it. And while they're at it they could do something about the snow. It's everywhere. The ground outside is completely covered and there is even more higher up, which could be dangerous. These places are dangerous enough without all that snow around. The council does not appear to have made any attempt to clear it. And another thing – I noticed some fairly large cliffs on the way here and found out later that there are no safety fences or nets. How silly can you get? You could have a pretty nasty fall up there. As soon as I get back I'm going to have a word with my local MP about all this.

26 January 1985

I write to warn of all who come here of great danger, increasing every day. It has come to my knowledge that a force greater than the mighty midge is about to seep over the Lairig Ghru. What may you ask is this abominable threat? Socks! Yes, nomadic socks have come to Scotland. Sabre-toothed stockings and ferocious ankle socks will cause terror across the Highlands. Watch out for the stripy ankle sock that lurks in these parts. It is the spawn of the Devil's Point. Be warned.

Melanie, 30 June 1996

The Pools of Dee,
What an amazing sight to see,
The fish are jumping,
My heart is pumping,
Oh no! I've been bitten by a flea.

Ben, 10 August 1997

Scottish topless netball team outing!

Amanda, Alice and Ruth, 9 June 2016

THE SPIRIT OF THE HILLS

WHILE SOME BOTHIERS turn to humour, others staying in the heart of the Cairngorms are moved to capture the spirit of such a wild place and its effect on them.

Alone I climb
The rugged hills that lead me out of time.

A London Scot 'on the tramp', 26 August 1928

When at long last I reach the end
And my heart steps out in vain
Leave me here by the mountain road
Never to wander again

By the mountain road, the open road
I will listen for the feet
Of those who love our own dear hills
And the mountain song so sweet.

29 March 1929

One of the most impressive sights I have ever seen in Scotland was a view of the Cairngorms from the doorway of the Corrour Bothy, an uninhabited shelter, situated near the foot of Devil's Point in Glen Dee.

When we arrived at this deserted dwelling, the glen was full of black swirling mists, and a cold stinging wind. A desolate, miserable looking place it seemed to us... However, we had an unexpected treat about three o'clock in the morning, when we went outside the bothy to have a look at the weather.

To our amazement, the scowling mists completely lifted, and Glen Dee lay bathed in glorious moonlight. There was a 'whisper on the nightwind', and away up yonder, amongst the stars, white shining mists hovered about the summit of Ben McDhui like clouds of incense.

I shall never forget the grandeur and serenity of that silvery view of the Cairngorm mountains, nor the stillness and peace, when we drank deep of its beauty.

> A Broughty Ferry Reader, 'Bonnie Scotland:
> The Cairngorms by Moonlight',
> *Dundee Evening Telegraph*, 18 July 1929

Beneath the letter the newspaper reports that 'Five shillings will be sent to the writer of the above.'

Came over from Aviemore with a 36lb pack, suffering great agony until I got used to it. Reached bothy soaked but made good meal and bedded down, assisted by the blankets left by some unknown comrade. I have felt exultant… on feeling the influence of the great corries.

> Archie Hunter, 22 June 1929

There is much comfort in High Hills,
And a great easing of the heart.

> 19 July 1929

These are the opening lines of a much-loved poem by Geoffrey Winthrop Young (1876–1958). Young was a poet and climber, later president of the Climbers' Club, who lost a leg during the First World War but carried on climbing with an artificial leg. The leg had various attachments for different rocks and ice, and in 1928 he climbed the Matterhorn.

Back once more amid the inimitable grandeur of the great Cairngorms, ample reward for the trials and tribulations of the guarding Lairig. Back from the crashing din and fumes of the city, to rest and gain courage for another year of strife, to lie by the doorway and send the imagination roaming the ridges and corries of the big tops, to feel the seductive confluence of rock castles and high snow fields.

> 22 June 1930

Magnificent scenery, enchanting mists – and soaking rain. What scenery, what weather! What pleasures can match those of the unorthodox insanities of the lovers of the high places, the

magnificent madness of the mountaineer? Yet thousands hit a pill
across a park or tup a hollow rubber sphere across a net and call it
sport! Ye Gods!

PE Shand, 21 July 1930

For go I must
But come I must
And if men ask you why,
You may put the blame
On the stars and the sun
And the dark hills and the sky.

Archie Hunter, 22 September 1930

Archibald Hunter was the nearest Corrour has come to having
a poet laureate. The surviving visitors' books contain many examples of his work (see following pages).

Back once more to Corrour, which I find silent and empty. Alone I sit
beside the fire and my thoughts shift over the hills. The wind is sighing
tonight and soughs round the bothy, while the infant Dee imitates
human voices as it flows down. Few realise how many more things
one sees and hears in the hills, alone. As I read this book, the shadowy
outline of past visitors seems to hover about then slowly fade. The
wind is rising, so I close tightly both the doors and replenish the dying
fire. The candles burn brightly while outside black night courses on.
Ere I sleep I must remember Byron, who once wrote:

Talk not to me of a name great in story,
The days of our youth are the days of our glory

G Miller, 19 October 1930

Had a very long lie and was only roused from the torpor which beset
me by the urgent craving for the commodities which collectively are
designated by the solitary word – breakfast... Cleaned the bothy
(my secret passion) and collected some more wood. Did practically
nothing all day and was consequently very tired.

Oh! To be in Corrour, now that July's here,
And whoever wakes in the bothy smells some essence of good cheer.
The Bantam coffee and bully beef,
The fragrance of tobacco leaf,

Whilst eagles devour their daily rations
During Seton Gordon's peregrinations.

Seton Gordon, 13 July 1931

'A Splendid Dream'

No lovelier hills than thine have laid
My tired thoughts to rest.
No joy of happier valleys made
Like peace within my breast.
Thine are the hills whereto my soul
Into the shadow creeps
To find a shelter clean and cool

And tranquil as a dream.

Archie Hunter, 13 July 1931

This is a re-worked version of a Walter de la Mare poem. Archie would record other versions of it in later visitors' books. Ironically, the original poem is entitled 'England'.

Let them drive in all their finery to their cities by the sea. Let them laugh at my greying unshaved visage. Let them stare with scorn as I eat my food and tear my bread with greasy hands. Let them turn in disdain as I hurl such curses at my primus stove. Let them build their promenades, their amusement palaces and their Towers of Babel. They vainly seek what I have found. For I have this day walked with the gods themselves.

14 July 1931

I have looked across the Dee, and there, with the sombre Devil's Point guarding, lay Corrour, and I am glad now that I have stopped, for the picture in every detail comes back to me, and indeed has never left me. Soon I stood at the door and drew my hands across the granite of the walls, and here I thanked Providence for the roughness of granite. I threw open the door and, stepping inside, drew in the intoxicating smell of the bothy... of visions of previous holidays... of happy hours on the hills... of struggles with Nature... It was a splendid dream.

Archie Hunter, 16 July 1931

May your heart keep true to the peaks above.
May your feet be sure on the hills you love.
May the summer mists and the winter storms
Ne'er hide your path to the High Cairngorms.

22 July 1931

There are other versions of this poem in the early visitors' books. It was written by John Campbell Shairp (1819–95), a pioneer environmentalist and champion of the Cairngorms who protested against the opening of the railway through Drumochter Pass. He held several academic posts, including Professor of Poetry at Oxford.

Over the hills, over the hills,
As high as the eagles rise;
To seek clear vision, wider views,
Beneath new skies.

Extract from Pilkington's 'Hills of Peace', D Mackenzie,
4 August 1931

Lawrence Pilkington (1855–1941), founder of the famous tile and pottery company, was also a writer and pioneer climber. Along with his brother Charles and local guide John Mackenzie, he made the first ascent of the Inaccessible Pinnacle on Skye in 1880. The quoted extract is from the poem 'Aspiration' in his recently published 1930 book *Hills of Peace*.

What joy the verdant glens to scour
And rocky corries by Corrour,
To climb while morning breezes cool
The crags and ridges of Cairn Toul,
To scan the Lairig far below
From wild Braeriach's wide plateau.
If it's to this your day's toil tends.
You have reward enough, my friends.

Douglas A Kidd, 11 August 1931

We must go east and west
We must go north and south
Till we find Heaven's door

Or we find Hell's mouth
We must travel all our days
The wide world over
And none shall understand our ways
But a fellow rover.

Excerpt from 'The Rover' by Archie Hunter, 22 August 1936

Charm of the Hills.
There is a strange quality about the hills which draws people from all walks of life to visit them. I am fortunate to be so blessed. This is my second summer here but not, I hope, the last. Cheerio.

A Tewnion, always a scout, 23 July 1938

From Ryvoan up to Corrour
When the hills the mist obscures
And the splendour of the pass is lost to you.
It makes you promise then
That you'll come back again
To see the wonders of the lofty Lairig Ghru.

JRB, 25 July 1938

Amid the Grampian mountains wild,
Where silence reigns supreme,
And nought disturbs the solitude,
Except the rushing stream,
There stands a lonely windswept house
Of no pretentious size.
But to the hail-slung mountaineer
It's perfect paradise.
No architectural beauties
It's crude grey walls adorn,
Yet wide its hospitable door
To high and lowly born.
Though meagre its capacities
Conveniences but few,
Its form is dear to all mankind
Who cross the Lairig Ghru.

Signed: Anonymous, 14 July 1939

After a warm night's rest we awoke to find the ground silver with
rime. The eastern sun was rising slowly and imperturbably down
the Devil's Point, bringing out in relief the yellows and duns, oranges
and browns of early autumn. Such intimate blendings of colour made
Gerald Manley Hopkins exclaim:

'Glory be to God for dappled things,
For skies of couple-colour as a brinded cow,
For rose-moles all in stipple on trout that swim.'

Leslie Bartlet, 23 September 1948

After the arduous trial of the Shelter Stone, the bothy comes like a
soothing balm to heal our sores and renew our limbs. To have battled
and [illegible], to stand at the doorway and drink in the grandeur of
the night. The moon silently riding in her 'silver shoon' above Macdhui.
The pale blue beauty drowning everything in its magic cloak as the
shadows rise into a peace that speaks of infinite rest. Death should
be like this. To come from the white-clad slopes of our beloved hills,
having drunk deep at the well of knowledge and beauty, and sit by
the fire until the spirit of the body entwines itself round our hearts.
To feel that we have worked and our wages are taken and to sink into
peaceful slumber in a place like this and know that we are not dead.

Archie Hunter, 3 January 1952

'Silver shoon' is a reference from Walter de la Mare's poem 'Silver'. Archie's companion notes more prosaically:

Archie is sitting beside me looking very downcast as he lost his pipe
on the hills and can't ruminate over his smoke. Am now going to
prepare our evening meal while the lad makes his entry.

WG Thompson, 3 January 1952

It haunts me here,
It haunts me there,
The Lairig haunts me everywhere.
If ever in heaven,
Or even in hell
I'll always be under the Lairig's spell.

James A Young (old customer), June 15, 1958

The sun highlights the sharp frozen edges of the Devil's Point, making it sparkle like a giant duodecagonal prism with truncated base and structured sides. My hand freezes as if seized by an emissary from the spirit world.

M Phillips, 2 November 1980

If I were to say that I was tired,
My knees were sore and soon retired,
It would sound like I had not enjoyed
Four days of walking in these wilds.
And if I were a dreamless man
I might be sat beside a fan,
Watching TV, night to night,
Getting fat on tasteless tripe.
But here I am in nature's place,
Getting cold, hot and wet, set by her pace,
I don't regret the sacrifice
Of energy, sweat and time.
For Scotland is a beautiful land,
The Highlands being the jewel in the crown.
I shall rejoice in life and while
I walk I have a song
Of travel, adventure, moving on.

Jo, 2 September 1998

Full of the joys of winter! A starlit start through the squeaking powder of the Lairig Ghru. The dawn catching the tops with the valleys full of mist below. Stomping a trail through the wind-smoothed drifts. Drawn to the temptations of the ice-rimmed Pools of Dee then a stride down to this glorious wee shelter for lunch and a nap. Onward onward into the winter's joy. What a world!

Tom, 12 February 2016

'It's funny how some distance makes everything seem small and the fears that once controlled me can't get to me at all. PS The cold never bothered me anyway.'

(from the Disney film Frozen)

Sarah, Sian, Alexandra, Mica, Johanna, Anna, 5 May 2016

I came back to the mountain not in search of anything in particular but only to be amongst them. Like an old friend who visits just to be in their presence.

Lundin, 31 May 2019

I LEAVE TONIGHT FROM EUSTON

I shall leave tonight from Euston
By the seven-thirty train
And from Perth in the early morning
I shall see the hills again.

From the top of Ben Macdhui
I shall watch the gathering storm
And see the crisp snow lying
At the back of Cairngorm.

I shall feel the mist from Bhrotain
And the pass by Lairig Ghru,
To look on dark Loch Einich
From the heights of Sgoran Dubh.

From the broken Barns of Bynack
I shall see the sunrise gleam
On the forehead of Ben Rinnes,
And Strathspey awake from dream.

And again in the dusk of evening
I shall find once more alone
The dark water of the Green Loch,
And the pass beyond Ryvoan.

For tonight I leave from Euston
And I leave the world behind;
Who has the hills as a lover
Will find them wondrous kind.

This elegiac poem was written by Ms AM Lawrence, who lived in Cumbria in the 1950s after spending part of her childhood in Nethy Bridge. It was found in Ryvoan Bothy and has become symbolic of the lure of the High Cairngorms and its bothies.

RANDOM THOUGHTS

ONE OF THE oldest verses in the visitors' books is an extract from an even older verse in SMCJ No 4, January 1897.

A mountain's a mountain in England. But when
The climber's in Scotland, it may be a Beinn,
A Creag or a Meall, a Spidean, a Sgor,
A Carn or a Monadh, a Stac or a Torr...

12 September 1929

HOWF RAL OVR FRAM HOWF ALSES FAM
HOWF AST HOWF LEIT OVR DAIE
HOWF IXED OVR FYTE IN FUTVR STATE
HOWF EW CYM BAC 2 SAIE.

19 September 1931

Some rhyme the bothy's name to lash,
Some rhyme the sunshine and the blast,
Some rhyme for want of grub and mash
And empty stomachs.
I rhyme the want of female lass
For empty hammocks

5 May 1932

[After a detailed account of a walk over Braeriach] I am afraid this report is rather long-winded, but as I am solo I have nothing else to do, so please forgive me this time. Goodnight.

TG Swanson, 3 July 1936

The following message is perhaps the most surreal of all the entries in the visitors' books.

If Mrs Hendry goes up Mount Everest she will be shocked to see 2
empty tins which I carelessly left there.

Winston Churchill, 24 July 1935

Did a little branding on the door. Visitors will please admire
said handiwork.

3 August 1936

Pioneer 1930s mountaineer WH Murray was among others
who carved their name at Corrour, but today such handiwork is
rightly regarded as vandalism.

A HAPPY NEW YEAR TO ALL WHO PASS THIS WAY, WHETHER
THEY BE HIKERS, CLIMBERS OR SANE PERSONS

1 January 1939

Depart Nottingham 12.58pm.
Arrive Corrour 10.05am.
The above service is a sad omission from the LMS timetable. Can
some plutocratic shareholder see that the matter is put right.

10 May 1940

The war-damaged London, Midland and Scottish Railway,
formed in 1923, was nationalised in 1948.

Back again! Where have I been meantime? Sure I don't know!

Dorothy L Johnson, 2 September 1940

Dorothy's companions have added 'I wish I knew' and 'I'm not
saying anything'.

Return of the Prodigal – this time with a wife! Last time was July
'43 when wives were considered an encumbrance in the hills. Now
I know better as we can do all the tramping we want to.

Mr and Mrs James HW Taylor, 18 August 1949

Dropped in a sharpened pencil on my way to Devil's Point and Cairn
Toul from Derry Lodge.

G Andrew, 20 December 1951

Lost in snowdrift – one two-man tent. Position approx. One mile due
south from this bothy, about 100 yards this side of river (ie between
river and Devil's Point). EITHER finder will keep OR would be most

grateful of return to following address… Reward of £2/o/o (present value of tent) and postage will be paid.

Lt Cdr JG Richards RN, 25 October 1956

Nothing to breathe but air,
Quick as a flash it's gone,
Nowhere to step on but off,
Nowhere to stand but on.

A MacLean, 28 September 1958

If anybody should find a canvas 'Bukta' water bucket near the White Bridge of Dee would they please post it to Mr D. Hamer… Thank you. PS It has twenty feet of nylon cord attached. Last seen floating near Chest of Dee. A REWARD will be forwarded to the finder. Postage refunded on application.

D Hame, 11 August 1959

It occurs to me that Corrour will provide future archaeologists with a unique opportunity for discovering long-lost facts concerning the twentieth century: 'Today we dug up from the floor of Corrour ruin an ice axe head circa 1960.'

21 May 1966

Climbing with friends a pleasure,
Climbing alone an education.

B Corbidge, 29 May 1972

We came, we saw, and we went back home.

FLM, 19 June 1977

Great place for a rock concert!

2 July 1977

TO HELP YOU IF IN NEED
I have hidden a five pound note somewhere in the bothy. See if you can find it.

Robin MacLean, 5 October 1977

I am looking for my pet gerbil. EDWIN is his name. If you find him please bring him home.

Millie, age 5, 23 March 1982

There is a pleasure in being here which nought but madmen know.

John Crossland, 11 October 1982

HELLO AND HELP

Mark fae Aberdeen, 3 July 1983

Bod an Deamhain. For Judith.

Ralph Storer, 8 June 1996

I am too tired to write anything right now.

14 June 1996

First time here in eighteen years. Am I really that old?

J Hunter Scone, 16 June 1996

I'm bloody knackered.

2 July 1996

Walked through from Coylumbridge carrying full pack. Last time I felt like this was when I was pregnant – at least I was able to take <u>off</u> my pack last night before crawling into tent outside!

Gilly, 8 July 1996

If you get bored, how many dolphins do you think you could fit in this bothy? Clue: average bottle-nosed dolphin is 3m long and you can stack them.

Gary, 23 August 1996

Jane met a new man, way out here in the middle of nowhere. If you can pull here, you can pull anywhere.

30 August 1998

Yet another function for a treasured 19th-century 'refuge in the wilderness' that, despite all the odds, abides into the third millennium.

Back again, this time doing research for my book on the history of the bothy. Who'd have thought, all those years ago?

Ralph Storer, 25 August 2019

Luath Press Limited

committed to publishing well written books worth reading

LUATH PRESS takes its name from Robert Burns, whose little collie Luath (*Gael.*, swift or nimble) tripped up Jean Armour at a wedding and gave him the chance to speak to the woman who was to be his wife and the abiding love of his life. Burns called one of the 'Twa Dogs' Luath after Cuchullin's hunting dog in Ossian's *Fingal*. Luath Press was established in 1981 in the heart of Burns country, and is now based a few steps up the road from Burns' first lodgings on Edinburgh's Royal Mile. Luath offers you distinctive writing with a hint of unexpected pleasures.

Most bookshops in the UK, the US, Canada, Australia, New Zealand and parts of Europe, either carry our books in stock or can order them for you. To order direct from us, please send a £sterling cheque, postal order, international money order or your credit card details (number, address of cardholder and expiry date) to us at the address below. Please add post and packing as follows: UK – £1.00 per delivery address; overseas surface mail – £2.50 per delivery address; overseas airmail – £3.50 for the first book to each delivery address, plus £1.00 for each additional book by airmail to the same address. If your order is a gift, we will happily enclose your card or message at no extra charge.

Luath Press Limited
543/2 Castlehill
The Royal Mile
Edinburgh EH1 2ND
Scotland
Telephone: +44 (0)131 225 4326 (24 hours)
Email: sales@luath. co.uk
Website: www. luath.co.uk